Dramascri

Treasure Island

ROBERT LOUIS STEVENSON

Dramatised by
David Calcutt

Nelson

Thomas Nelson & Sons Ltd
Nelson House
Mayfield Road
Walton-on-Thames
Surrey KT12 5PL
United Kingdom

Treasure Island – the script © David Calcutt 1999
The right of David Calcutt to be identified as author of this play has been asserted by
David Calcutt in accordance with the Copyright, Design and Patents Act 1988.
All applications to perform this play should be addressed in the first instance to the
Royalty and Permissions Department, ITPS Ltd, Cheriton House, North Way, Andover,
Hampshire SP10 5BE (*Telephone* 01264 342756; *Fax* 01264 342792).

Introduction, activities and explanatory notes © Thomas Nelson 1999

Designed and produced by Bender Richardson White
Typesetting by Malcolm Smythe
Cover illustration by Dave Grimwood
Black and white illustrations by John James
Printed by L. Rex Printing Co. Ltd., China

This edition published by Thomas Nelson & Sons Ltd 1999.
ISBN 0–17–432560–6
9 8 7 6 5 4 3 2
03   02   01   00   99

CONTENTS

SERIES EDITOR'S INTRODUCTION

Dramascripts is an exciting series of plays especially chosen for students in the lower and middle years of secondary school. The titles range from the best in modern writing to adaptations of classic texts such as *A Christmas Carol* and *Silas Marner*.

Dramascripts can be read or acted purely for the enjoyment and stimulation that they provide; however, each play in the series also offers all the support that pupils need in working with the text in the classroom:

● **Introduction** – this offers important background information and explains something about the ways in which the play came to be written.

● **Script** – this is clearly set out in ways that make the play easy to handle in the classroom.

● **Notes** explain references that pupils might not understand, and language points that are not obvious.

● **Activities** – at the end of scenes, acts or sections – give pupils the opportunity to explore the play more fully. Types of activity include: discussion, writing, hot-seating, improvisation, acting, freeze-framing, story-boarding and artwork.

● **Looking Back at the Play** – this section has further activities for more extended work on the play as a whole with emphasis on characters, plots, themes and language.

INTRODUCTION
BY DAVID CALCUTT

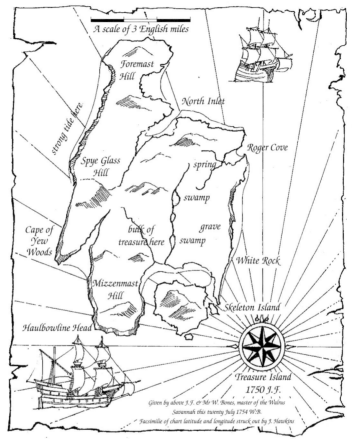

A scale of 3 English miles

Foremast Hill

North Inlet

strong tide here

Roger Cove

Spye Glass Hill

spring

swamp

Cape of Yew Woods

bulk of treasure here

grave swamp

White Rock

Mizzenmast Hill

Skeleton Island

Haulbowline Head

Treasure Island
1750 J.F.

Given by above J.F. & Mr W. Bones, master of the Walrus
Savannah this twenty July 1754 W.B.
Facsimilie of chart latitude and longitude struck out by J. Hawkins

From when I first read it as a child, *Treasure Island* has always been one of my favourite books. Its scenes and characters have haunted my imagination and my dreams since then, and, for me, the whole story has that larger-than-life quality, that sense of having a life and vitality of its own, outside the pages of the book, that all great stories have. And, when I came to work on this adaptation, it was that dream-like, and at times, nightmarish quality, that suggested the entire structure to me.

For, although *Treasure Island* is a very good adventure story, it's also, I think, more than that. It's a journey, not only across the sea to an island in search of treasure, but a journey out of the ordinary, everyday world, into the world of the strange, the terrifying, and the fantastic – a journey into our own dream world, in fact.

Or into our own past. For stories of journeys and quests are among the oldest in the world. They go back to our own very beginnings, before we settled down into farming communities, when we were still a nomadic people, wandering the world, always moving on from one new place to another, and having to overcome the hardships and dangers and terrors that we encountered on the way. And each time we came to some new place, and overcame some new danger, we learned something more about ourselves. So it's that, I believe, that appeals to us in stories such as *Treasure Island*.

For they too, in the course of the journey they take us on, tell us something about ourselves, reveal truths about the human heart that add to our stock of self-understanding. In the case of this story, those truths aren't very pleasant. For, once we're on the island, we see human beings as they can be at their worst – treacherous, murderous, greedy, savage killers.

But, to counterbalance this, there's also a sense of freedom and liberation, the sheer joy of life and adventure, that's embodied in the figure of Long John Silver. He rises above all the nastiness and cruelty, part of it himself, but also a kind of answer to it in the very hugeness of his spirit, his capacity for living life to the full. And this is the treasure that we discover at the end of the journey, this is the gold we bring back with us – the knowledge that life is there to be lived in all its glory, if only we have the courage to take it on. This is the challenge Silver throws down to Jim, and us, at the very end of the play, when his cry rings out, echoing through our dreams: 'Pieces of eight'.

CASTING

Apart from two female characters in the play (and one of those does not appear in the book), all are male. At first, this might seem to present difficulties when casting the play for production in a mixed school or youth theatre. However, it's the playwright's feeling that parts should be cast according to the ability of the actor, rather than their sex, age, or race. There should be no difficulty in casting girls in any of the roles, as long as they are happy for that to happen.

THE SET

One of the aims in writing this play was to create a piece of theatre that was fast-moving, where scenes flowed easily and quickly from one to the other. Because of this, it would seem to make sense not to try to create any realistic set. The constant bringing on and off of props, and the changing of scenery, would delay the action, and also act against any sense of the whole thing being a fantastic, larger-than-life, dream world.

The playwright's suggestion for any production is that there is a single set, with one or two raised areas, composed largely of boxes, chests, barrels, pieces of timber, rope, and sheets or canvas. This jumble of odds and ends could then be used to create, simply, efficiently, and effectively, the various locations in the play – the inn, the Bristol docks, the deck of the *Hispaniola,* the stockade, the island, and so on. And again, rather than interrupt the flow of the play, these locations would be created by the actors themselves, in full view of the audience, as part of the action. For, in theatre, all that you see and hear should be part of, and integral to, the drama.

David Calcutt

THE CHARACTERS

ADULT JIM Jim as a young man, and the narrator of this story

IN DEVON

JIM HAWKINS a boy, aged about 15, impetuous and longs for adventure

MRS HAWKINS Jim's mother, a widow, in her mid-30s, keeper of *The Admiral Benbow Inn*, hard-working, level-headed and loving

THE CAPTAIN also known as Billy Bones, one of Flint's crew, loud-mouthed, blustering, and addicted to drinking rum

BLACK DOG one of Flint's crew, unpleasant, mean, cowardly

BLIND PEW one of Flint's crew, sadistic, cruel

DOCTOR LIVESEY the local doctor and magistrate, middle-aged, sensible and rational

SQUIRE TRELAWNEY the local squire and landowner, middle-aged, well-meaning, good-hearted, but rather self-important and foolhardy

HUNTER the Squire's servant, faithful to the end

6 LOCAL VILLAGERS

AT BRISTOL

LONG JOHN SILVER also known as *Barbecue*, Flint's ex-quartermaster, now keeper of *The Spyglass Inn*, in his 50s, clever, commanding, treacherous, murderous, brave, self-seeking, humourous, sly, quick-witted, strong, and physically agile, despite lacking a leg.

REBECCA SILVER Silver's wife, about the same age, and temperament as her husband

GEORGE MERRY one of Flint's crew, envious of Silver

TOM MORGAN one of Flint's crew, not very bright

CAPTAIN SMOLLETT the captain of the *Hispaniola*, middle-aged, shrewd, plain-spoken, stiff

ON THE HISPANIOLA

ISRAEL HANDS Flint's ex-gunner, clever and cruel

REDCAP one of Flint's crew

DICK an ordinary sailor, in his early 20s, persuaded by Silver to join the mutineers

6 SAILORS

ON THE ISLAND

BEN GUNN one of Flint's crew, marooned on the island for three years, and therefore rather eccentric, with a longing for cheese

GRAY an ordinary sailor, loyal to Captain Smollett

JOYCE an ordinary sailor, loyal to Captain Smollett

6 ISLAND VOICES *Note: The 6 locals, sailors and 'island voices' can be played by the same actors.*

TREASURE ISLAND
THE MAP
ACT 1 ❖ SCENE 1

The BOY JIM is curled asleep on the floor, amongst a jumble of ropes, sheets, boxes, and timber. JIM, as an adult, enters from one side, slowly, and crosses to stand near his childhood self. He speaks to the audience.

ADULT JIM   At night, still, I dream of those old times, and our   1
nightmare voyage to that accursed island. Even though
many years have passed, the figures that haunted my days
when I was a boy return, with the sun's going down, to
haunt me again. And that isle of treasure is once more my
only world, and I'm lost there, marooned. But not alone.

*(The CHORUS appear, as figures in JIM's nightmare, moving
forward through the dark to stand around him.)*

With the coming of the dark, figures walk from the
shadows, the ragged figures of men long dead – hanged or   10
shot or drowned in the deep – rising up now out of the
black waves. And I hear once more the sounds of the
sea . . .

1st FIGURE   Crash of waves on the rocks.

2nd FIGURE   Boom of surf on the shore.

3rd FIGURE   Sail-slap . . .

4th FIGURE   Wind-crack . . .

 that accursed island *This opening phrase in the play is taken from the final paragraph of the book.*

5th FIGURE	Like a gunshot echoing through the jungle trees . . .
6th FIGURE	And the shrieking of birds like souls damned in hell.
ADULT JIM	And I hear too the voices of men, dry as rat's feet scuttling over dead men's bones, whispering the words of that nightmare song.

20

(All figures chant, in a hoarse, terrifying whisper. The BOY JIM begins to stir restlessly in his sleep.)

ALL	Fifteen men on a dead man's chest Yo ho ho and a bottle of rum Drink and the devil had done for the rest Yo ho ho and a bottle of rum.

(The first line of the chant is repeated over, growing louder each time.)

30

Fifteen men on a dead man's chest . . . , etc.

(At the final line, the figure of SILVER suddenly appears, on a raised area, he cries out.)

SILVER	Pieces of eight, Jim! Pieces of eight!

(BOY JIM wakes with a gasp and stares up at SILVER.)

DISCUSSION Opening scenes in a play are of great importance. They must capture the audience's attention immediately, and set the tone, style and atmosphere for the whole play.

As a class, discuss what effects you think the playwright is trying to create in this opening scene, and how he's trying to capture the audience's attention.

● What does this short opening scene tell us about the play that is to follow?

ACT 1 ❖ SCENE 2

Immediately, MRS HAWKINS enters, carrying a crate of bottles. She speaks sharply to JIM. JIM turns to her. SILVER goes. ADULT JIM moves to one side.

MRS HAWKINS   On your feet, Jim! Look at you, daydreaming there, and   1
with all this work to be done.

(JIM jumps to his feet. MRS HAWKINS puts the crate down.)

You can start by setting the tables. And when you've done
that you can put the sign up outside. Let people know we're
open for business again.

JIM   Yes, mother.

*(JIM begins to set out the interior of the inn. MRS HAWKINS
lays out the bottles from the crate. The CHORUS now enter as
LOCALS. As they speak, they help to create the interior of the*   10
inn, setting out tables, stools, a simple doorway, and so on.)

1st LOCAL   The year of grace, 1756 . . .

2nd LOCAL   A fair morning, when the sun's high and bright . . .

3rd LOCAL   Near a village on the Devon coast . . .

4th LOCAL   On a headland rising above the sea . . .

5th LOCAL   The place of his birth and growing up . . .

6th LOCAL   And the place where all his bad dreams begin.

(MRS HAWKINS speaks to JIM.)

MRS HAWKINS   Jim. The sign.

1756 *The actual year in which the novel is set is not given in the book. But
the date when Flint gave the map to the Captain (Billy Bones) is given on a
map of the island as 'July 10th 1754'. (See* Looking Back at the Play
section.)

(JIM takes up The Admiral Benbow *sign, climbs the central*   20
*raised area, and hangs the sign from a pole. The LOCALS
continue creating the inn. ADULT JIM narrates.)*

ADULT JIM   I was fourteen years old, and lived with my mother at the
inn we kept on a headland above the coast, *The Admiral
Benbow.* A lonely part of the country, it was, and lonelier to
me at that time, since the death of my father just a few
weeks before.

(The LOCALS speak, leaving on their lines.)

1st LOCAL   A sad day that was for us all when he died.

2nd LOCAL   A good man, he was, and well-liked.   30

3rd LOCAL   Honest too, and he kept a fine alehouse.

4th LOCAL   But death is death, and life must go on.

5th LOCAL   And it's good to see the place opening up again.

6th LOCAL   For the nights have been cold and dark, without *The
Admiral* to bring us some cheer.

MRS HAWKINS   I only hope I can keep it going. There's little enough in the
way of hard cash my poor husband left behind him.

*(MRS HAWKINS finishes setting out bottles and glasses, and JIM
finishes fixing the sign. He remains there, gazing out.)*

ADULT JIM   There was little cheer for us, with my father's death, and   40
the expense of his funeral. Whether we could continue in
our livelihood we still weren't sure. And autumn was here,
bringing the bad weather – rain, storm, and high winds.
And that year, it wasn't only the bad weather it brought.

(From the raised area, JIM calls out.)

The Admiral Benbow *Admiral Benbow was a famous British naval officer.
The inn is named after him.*

JIM	There's somebody coming! Up the path from the cove!
MRS HAWKINS	Who?
JIM	I don't know. Never seen him before. Looks like a seafaring man. He's tall . . . and he's got a pigtail . . .
MRS HAWKINS	All right. Come down, now, Jim.

50

(JIM stays where he is.)

JIM	You think it might be our first customer?
MRS HAWKINS	Maybe. And I hope not the last. And that he's got hard cash to pay his way. Come down, I said.

(JIM drops down from the raised level, just as the CAPTAIN enters, carrying a small chest in one hand. Startled, the CAPTAIN grabs hold of JIM. They freeze as ADULT JIM narrates.)

ADULT JIM	And I remember him as if it were yesterday, that man from the sea, with his filthy coat and his ragged hands and his broken nails . . . and a haunted, hunted look on his face, like a creature fleeing from all the devils of the world.

60

(Characters unfreeze.)

CAPTAIN	This your grog-shop, is it, boy?
JIM	Yes, sir . . .
CAPTAIN	Who keeps it? Your father?

(MRS HAWKINS steps forward.)

. . . he's got a pigtail . . . *It was an old and common tradition for sailors to wear their hair in a pigtail, which was bound tightly with twine covered in tar. This was the reason, incidentally, sailors also became known as 'tars'.*

grog-shop *Strictly speaking, 'grog' was a mixture of rum, warm water and lemon, but it became a general term among sailors for rum. So, the 'grog-shop' is the inn.*

MRS HAWKINS	No. I do. His mother. What is it you want?
	(*The CAPTAIN looses JIM, and speaks to MRS HAWKINS.*)
CAPTAIN	What do I want? Rum, that's what. Give me a glass of rum.
MRS HAWKINS	Jim. Pour the gentleman a glass of rum.
	(*JIM goes to the counter, fills a glass with rum and takes it to the CAPTAIN.*)
JIM	Here's your rum, sir.
	(*The CAPTAIN takes the glass, and drinks the rum in one go. He holds the glass out.*)
CAPTAIN	Another.
	(*JIM takes the glass, refills it, and brings it back. The CAPTAIN takes it, sipping at it this time, and looking around at the inn.*)
	This is a handy cove. And a pleasant-situated grog-shop. I've heard it well-spoke of. Much company, is there?
MRS HAWKINS	Very little, more's the pity.
CAPTAIN	Well, then. This is the berth for me. I'll stay here a bit. I'm a plain man. Rum and eggs and bacon is what I want. And that headland up there for to watch ships off.
MRS HAWKINS	As you plan to be our guest, what might we call you?
CAPTAIN	You might call me Captain.
MRS HAWKINS	Very well, Captain. Perhaps we can do business.
CAPTAIN	I see what you're after. (*He takes some coins from his pocket and slaps them on the table.*) Enough, is it?
	(*MRS HAWKINS takes up the coins.*)
MRS HAWKINS	It'll do, for now.
CAPTAIN	Good. Now, stow my chest in my berth and bring me some more rum. The whole bottle.

70

80

90

*(He puts the chest down and sits at one of the tables.
MRS HAWKINS takes the chest off. JIM takes the bottle and sets
it down on the table.)*

CAPTAIN   What's your name, boy?

JIM   Jim, sir.

CAPTAIN   Jim. You seem a sharp enough lad. *(He takes out a coin and*   100
slaps it on the table.) You see that, Jim? That's a silver
fourpenny. Now, you keep a weather-eye open for any
seafaring men that might come this way, and it's yours.
And you'll get one like it the first of every month. You
understand?

JIM   I'm to keep a look-out for any seafaring men.

CAPTAIN   That's right.

JIM   And if one should enquire after you. . . ?

CAPTAIN   You tell them nothing! You don't know me! Never seen me!
Have you got that clear?   110

JIM   Yes.

CAPTAIN   Good. Go on, then, Jim. Take it.

(JIM goes to take the coin. The CAPTAIN grabs his hand.)

And, mind, in particular, you keep your eyes sharp for a
seafaring man with one leg. The minute you clap eyes on
the likes of him, you let me know. Right?

(JIM nods. The CAPTAIN releases his hand.)

Good. We're all square. Now, go on about your business,
and leave me to my rum.

a seafaring man with one leg *not so unusual then as it might sound to
us now. During the 18th Century, Britain was becoming a great sea-power,
and many men serving at sea lost limbs in naval battles.*

(JIM takes the coin, turns, and goes across to the counter. The **120**
CAPTAIN speaks, partly to JIM, partly to himself.)

A seafaring man with one leg. He's the devil to keep watch
for. The devil himself, climbed straight out of hell.

(He drinks, then sits with head bowed, over the bottle.)

DISCUSSION We find out in this scene that Jim's father is dead, but
we're not told how he died.
    In small groups, discuss how you think his father did die, and what
effect his death has had on Jim and his mother.

STORYBOARDING There have been several film versions of *Treasure Island*.
Imagine that you are filming the opening of the story. Choose four key events
from Scene 2 and storyboard them: sketch what you would show in each frame;
write notes on what the audience might hear over the image, and make notes on
what the camera is doing. For example, one frame might show the Captain
walking up the path towards the inn.
    We would hear the sound of the sea below, gulls crying, a gentle wind
blowing.
    The camera would show the Captain in long shot first, walking towards the
camera, and then perhaps zoom in for a close-up of his face, as he stops, and
looks back suspiciously.

WRITING Imagine you're Jim, watching the Captain approach along the path to
the inn. Write down your thoughts as you watch him approach.

ACTING In twos or threes, create a short scene in which Mrs Hawkins tells one or
two of the locals about her new guest at the inn, and what she thinks of him.

ACT 1 ❖ SCENE 3

ADULT JIM | I kept watch for him as he asked. And though in the weeks 1
that followed, a few seamen did sometimes stop by, I never
saw any man with one leg – except in my worst dreams. As
for the Captain, he was a silent man, mostly, keeping
himself to himself, hardly speaking even when spoken to,
just looking up, fierce and sudden, with a glare in his eyes
that froze your soul. So, people learned to leave him be.
And whatever secrets he may have carried within him, were
locked as fast as the chest he kept stored in his room.

(LOCALS enter again, on their lines, speaking to the audience 10
and each other. MRS HAWKINS also enters.)

(The LOCALS gradually take their places at the tables, and JIM
and his mother serve them with bottles, glasses, and so on.)

1st LOCAL | We don't even know his name . . .

2nd LOCAL | Nor where he comes from, or what he wants here.

3rd LOCAL | Spends his days skulking around up there on the
headland.

4th LOCAL | And his nights in here, drinking rum.

5th LOCAL | And making us listen to those stories of his . . .

6th LOCAL | Tales of battles at sea and bloody deeds . . . 20

1st LOCAL | Hangings and shootings and walking the plank . . .

2nd LOCAL | Storms and high winds, hurricanes and shipwrecks . . .

---

 walking the plank *A punishment favoured by pirates. A plank of wood*
was extended out from the side of the ship, and the victim was made to walk
along it, blindfolded and with hands tied behind his back, until he fell off the
end and into the sea.

3rd LOCAL	And wild places out on the Spanish Main.
	(The CAPTAIN looks up and calls out.)
CAPTAIN	This bottle's empty! Bring me another!
	(Everyone falls silent. He calls again.)
	Did you hear me? More rum, I said!
	(MRS HAWKINS turns to him, sharply.)
MRS HAWKINS	I heard you. But I have other people to serve . . .
CAPTAIN	You'll serve me when I call for it! Bring me more rum.
	(MRS HAWKINS goes to the counter, takes up a bottle and glass.)
MRS HAWKINS	A glass, is it?
CAPTAIN	The bottle.
	(MRS HAWKINS puts the glass down, takes the bottle across to the table and puts it down firmly in front of him. Then she turns and goes back to serving the others. The CAPTAIN drinks heavily from the bottle as LOCALS talk, across each other)
4th LOCAL	He has the look of a man who's seen wicked things.
MRS HAWKINS	Yes, and done some as well, I've no doubt.
5th LOCAL	A man with secrets, a man on the run.
6th LOCAL	And waiting here for his past to catch up with him.
	(The CAPTAIN begins to sing, drunkenly.)
CAPTAIN	Sixteen men on a dead man's chest Yo ho ho, and a bottle of rum

30

40

The Spanish Main *Originally, this was the name given to the mainland of Spanish America. It was later expanded to include the whole area of the Caribbean where, from the 16th to the 18th Centuries, acts of piracy were widespread.*

Drink and the devil had done for the rest
Yo ho ho and a bottle of rum.

(He glares round at the LOCALS.)

What's the matter with you? Sing out! You've heard it
before! Come on! Sing out, you lubbers! 50

*(The CAPTAIN sings again, louder. Half-heartedly, some of the
LOCALS join in with him.)*

Sixteen men on a dead man's chest
Yo ho ho . . .

(He stops, roars at the LOCALS.)

I can't hear you! Sing out, I said! Let me hear your voices.
Or I'll have every man jack of you walking the plank!

*(He begins again, beating time on the table. The LOCALS all
join in. DOCTOR LIVESEY enters, unnoticed by the CAPTAIN.)*

CAPTAIN/LOCALS Sixteen men on a dead man's chest 60
Yo ho ho and a bottle of rum
Drink and the devil had done for the rest
Yo ho ho and a bottle of rum!

(At the end of the song he calls out.)

CAPTAIN That's enough! No more! No more of that! Stop your
tongues, now. Give me some peace and quiet!

*(He drinks and slouches forward. DOCTOR LIVESEY approaches
MRS HAWKINS.)*

MRS HAWKINS Doctor Livesey. It's a pleasure to see you here. Will you take
something? 70

DOCTOR LIVESEY Some ale, if you'd be so kind, Mrs Hawkins.

lubbers *An insulting term. Sailors often referred to those who weren't sailors
as 'land-lubbers'. Lubber comes from the Medieval word 'loby', meaning
someone who was clumsy or ungainly.*

(MRS HAWKINS draws him a mug of ale.)

I was just returning from my rounds, and I thought I would take the opportunity of stopping off to enquire . . .

(The CAPTAIN calls out, not looking up.)

CAPTAIN   Quiet, I said!

(There is a moment's pause, then DOCTOR LIVESEY continues speaking to MRS HAWKINS.)

LIVESEY   . . . to enquire after yourself and your son.

MRS HAWKINS   I'm much obliged to you, Doctor. We're both well, thank you.   80

LIVESEY   Good. I'm glad to hear it. *(He raises his mug.)* Your health, Mrs . . .

(The CAPTAIN looks up and roars out.)

CAPTAIN   Silence there, between decks!

(Angrily, DOCTOR LIVESEY thumps his mug down and turns to face the CAPTAIN.)

LIVESEY   Were you addressing me, sir?

CAPTAIN   Yes, sir, I was, damn your eyes!

(LIVESEY approaches the CAPTAIN.)   90

LIVESEY   Then I have only one thing to say to you, sir! That if you keep on drinking rum as you do, the world will soon be quit of a very dirty scoundrel!

(In rage, the CAPTAIN leaps to his feet, drawing a knife from his belt and pointing it at LIVESEY.)

CAPTAIN   You dog . . . !

the world will soon be quit of a very dirty scoundrel *The Doctor's practised eye can already see that rum is killing the Captain.*

LIVESEY	I'll have you know that I'm not only a doctor, but also a magistrate, and if you do not put that knife away this instant, I promise you that you will hang at the next assizes!

100

(Pause.)

CAPTAIN	A magistrate.

(He lowers the knife and puts it in his belt.)

I want no trouble.

LIVESEY	I'm glad to hear it. But now that I know there's such as you in my district, I shall keep close watch on you. And if I catch a breath of complaint, I'll take the means to have you hunted down and routed out! You can rely upon it!

(He turns from the CAPTAIN, goes to the counter, takes up his mug again.)

110

LIVESEY	Your good health, Mrs Hawkins.

(He drains the mug, places it down.)

And now, good night to you. And to you, Jim. I shall make certain of stopping by again in the not too distant future. You can be certain of it.

MRS HAWKINS	Good night, Doctor. And thank you.

(LIVESEY bows his head and turns to the rest of the LOCALS.)

LIVESEY	A good night to you all.

(He goes.)

(The CAPTAIN turns and glares at everyone, then picks up his

120

magistrate . . . assizes *A magistrate had (and still has) the power of arrest and trying cases of minor offences. Every so often a visiting Judge would arrive in small towns and villages to try more serious cases. These were known as the 'assizes'.*

bottle, drinks heavily from it, slams it on the table, and walks off to stand apart. MRS HAWKINS turns to the LOCALS.)

MRS HAWKINS It's late. Finish your drinks. I'm closing.

(The LOCALS finish their drinks and, one by one, leave the inn. JIM and his mother clear up.)

MRS HAWKINS That godless man'll be the ruin of us, Jim. I swear he will. How much longer I can put him with him staying here, I don't know. It's not for the money. What he gave me was used up weeks ago. And if I ask him for more he just gives me . . . one of them looks of his. Curse the man! I wish I knew a way of being rid of him! 130

JIM Don't say that mother!

MRS HAWKINS What? You're speaking up for him?

JIM He's not a bad man – at least, he may have been once, but now . . . now I think he's just scared.

MRS HAWKINS Scared, is he? He scares our customers, sure enough.

JIM Not enough that they don't come back every night. It seems to me he brings a bit of excitement to their lives . . .

MRS HAWKINS It's the kind of excitement I could do without. And the sooner he's gone from here, the happier I'll be. He's like a 140 bad dream. A bad dream come to life, and walking out in broad daylight.

(She goes, leaving JIM alone.)

ARTWORK Make a sketch of how you think the interior of the inn might look on stage. Choose one moment from Scene 3 and decide where you might position the characters, and what scenery and props there might be.

In small groups, compare your sketches, and discuss the difference.

LANGUAGE Look at the Captain's language. How does the way he speaks tell us something about the kind of character he is? Make a note of all the non-standard words and phrases he uses. How can you tell from his speech that he's spent much of his life at sea?

FREEZE FRAMING Make a freeze-frame of the moment in Scene 3 just after Doctor Livesey leaves the inn. Speak aloud the thoughts of each character in the scene at that moment.

You could also make a sketch of this moment, with a thought-bubble for each character.

ACTING Create a short scene in which some of the locals who were present at the inn in Scene 3 discuss the events of the evening, perhaps relating them to some who weren't there.

Try to give each character in the scene a slightly different point of view of the events, and the characters of the Doctor and the Captain.

LANGUAGE As an educated man, Doctor Livesey speaks in a precise and formal way, even when he's angry. Have a good look at the way the Doctor speaks, and then write a letter from the Doctor to his friend Squire Trelawney (who will appear later in the play), in which he tells him about the Captain, describes his character, and relates the events of their meeting at the inn.

DISCUSSION As a class, discuss all the reasons you can think of as to why Jim is sympathetic towards the Captain. Look at the text, and see if you can find anything there to support your views.

ACT 1 ❖ SCENE 4

ADULT JIM comes forward. As he speaks, the CAPTAIN climbs up to a raised area, and gazes out, as if to sea. BOY JIM moves to stand beneath the raised area, also gazing out.

ADULT JIM   If he was a bad dream, he wasn't the worst. There's one I   1
remember in particular. I'm standing on the headland, looking out to sea. It's night, and everything about me is black. The land, the sky, the sea, all cloaked in blackness.

(YOUNG JIM speaks, in his dream.)

JIM   A cold wind rustles in the grasses. The surf washes over the rocks below. The cries of strange birds lift up out of the dark.

ADULT JIM   Then the cloud breaks and rolls away, and there's the full
moon glittering on the waves. And out there, in the middle   10
of the ocean, lit by the moonlight, a ship.

JIM   Its sails hang in tatters. Its masts are cracked. Its sides shine, white as bone.

ADULT JIM   And on its deck stands a single figure, tall and gaunt, a figure with one leg, shrouded in rags, and as the ship draws closer towards the shore, it raises its hands and pulls back its hood . . .

JIM   And its hands are claws and I can see its face . . .

ADULT JIM   And its face is a skull and it speaks my name!

(BLACK DOG enters, suddenly.)   20

BLACK DOG   Jim? Jim, is it? Is that your name, lad?

(JIM turns to BLACK DOG with a start. We are back in the inn, now, a little while later.)

JIM   Yes. But how did you . . . ?

BLACK DOG	That's what they told me down in the village there. Mrs Hawkins and her son, Jim. Keep *The Admiral Benbow* inn. I'm right, am I?
JIM	Yes . . .
BLACK DOG	A fine establishment, they said. It looks fine enough. My mate, Bill. He has lodgings here, does he?
JIM	Bill?
BLACK DOG	Billy Bones.
JIM	There is someone staying here . . . But he calls himself the Captain . . .
BLACK DOG	The Captain! Oh, yes. That's my mate, Bill, that is. He'd call himself the Captain. Here, is he?
JIM	Not at the moment. He's out – walking – but he's likely to be back soon.
BLACK DOG	Good. Bring me some rum. I'll wait here for him. Yes. I'll wait and give my good mate Bill a pleasant surprise.

30

40

(JIM fetches BLACK DOG a glass of rum.)

(BLACK DOG drinks.)

You seem a good lad. A good son to your mother, are you? Yes. Her pride and joy. I've a son of my own. He's the pride of my heart. Like you, he is. But I'll tell you, Jim, the great things for boys is discipline. You take my meaning? That's what makes a boy, that's what gives him backbone. Discipline.

(The CAPTAIN has come down from the raised area and now stands at the doorway. JIM sees him.)

50

JIM	Captain . . .

(BLACK DOG turns and sees the CAPTAIN.)

BLACK DOG	Bill! Here you are! You know me, don't you, Bill? You know your old shipmate.

CAPTAIN	Black Dog!
BLACK DOG	Yes. Black Dog as ever was, come to see his old mate Billy Bones at *The Admiral Benbow* inn.
CAPTAIN	So. You've run me down. Well, then. Here I am. Speak up. What is it you want?
BLACK DOG	You know what it is we want, Bill. But we shouldn't speak of it in front of the lad. *(He turns to JIM, speaks sharply.)* You there. Out of it. Go on. And none of your keyholes, neither.

(JIM starts to move away, as BLACK DOG turns back to the CAPTAIN.)

Now, Billy, let's sit down and talk square like old . . .

(The CAPTAIN suddenly draws his cutlass.)

CAPTAIN	No!

(He brings the cutlass down on a table with a crash. BLACK

and none of your keyholes neither *Black Dog is warning Jim not to eavesdrop on their conversation.*

60

DOG jumps back in fear.)

BLACK DOG   Now, Billy . . .   70

(The CAPTAIN advances around the table towards BLACK DOG, threatening him with the cutlass. BLACK DOG dodges around the tables and stools.)

CAPTAIN   There's but one thing you'll get from me, Black Dog!

BLACK DOG   There ain't just me to deal with . . .

CAPTAIN   I'll run you through . . .

BLACK DOG   You ain't Silver, Billy . . . !

CAPTAIN   And you ain't Flint!

BLACK DOG   Play fair with us, Bill. Play fair with your old mates, or we'll see you swing!   80

CAPTAIN   See me swing, will you! If it comes to swinging, then swing all, I say!

(The CAPTAIN raises his cutlass to strike at black dog. BLACK DOG screams out. As the CAPTAIN swings the cutlass down it strikes against the sign. The CAPTAIN stumbles, and BLACK DOG escapes. The CAPTAIN calls after him.)

Swing all! You hear me! I'll see you all in hell, damn and blast your souls. Every last dog of you!

(The CAPTAIN stumbles again. JIM moves towards him.)

JIM   Captain . . .   90

CAPTAIN   I'm all right, boy – I'll be all right . . .

JIM   Sit down . . .

CAPTAIN   Get me some rum – some rum's what I want . . .

 or we'll see you swing *Black Dog is threatening to turn the Captain over to the authorities, and have him hanged.*

JIM	You shouldn't . . .
CAPTAIN	Rum! A glass of rum, boy, or you'll know the worst of it . . . !
	(He grabs hold of a table and sits, heavily.)
	For mercy's sake, Jim, one glass . . .
JIM	All right. One glass, and no more.
	(JIM pours a glass of rum and brings it to the CAPTAIN. The CAPTAIN drinks it down, greedily. He speaks, half to himself, half to JIM.)
CAPTAIN	If you'd seen the things I've seen . . . been in the places I've been in . . . hot as pitch and men dropping with the Yellow Jack . . . and the land heaving and pitching like the sea . . . I've lived on rum – it's been meat and drink, and man and wife to me . . .
JIM	That man. Who was he?
CAPTAIN	Black Dog? A cut-throat and a coward. But not the worst of them. Oh, no. There's a lot worse than Black Dog. And they've got the wind of me. They've run me down and found me out. But I'm not afraid of them! I'll shake them again, so I will!
JIM	Who? Who are they?
CAPTAIN	Flint's men, what's left of them. That's who they are. You heard of him, have you, boy? You heard of Flint?
	(MRS HAWKINS has entered, and heard the last part of this speech)
MRS HAWKINS	I've heard of him. *(She approaches.)* I saw the commotion as I was coming back up from the village. And that man

100

110

120

Yellow Jack *Slang term for Yellow Fever, a tropical virus disease accompanied by jaundice, turning the victim's skin yellow.*

	running from the inn. *(To the Captain.)* So this is more trouble you've brought on us. And it's not the last of it, either, I'm thinking. This Flint. He was a pirate, wasn't he?
CAPTAIN	A devil is what he was. The darkest-hearted devil that ever walked land or sailed sea. Dead, now. At least I thought he was. But sometimes I see him still. Sometimes at night I get the horrors, and I see him there, in the corner, grinning – give me some more rum . . .
MRS HAWKINS	No! No more!
CAPTAIN	Damn you . . . !
MRS HAWKINS	And damn you for the evil you've brought here and the money you owe!
CAPTAIN	Money, is it? I'll pay what I owe, and more, just give me a glass of rum . . .
MRS HAWKINS	The way you look, Captain, another glass, and it'll be the death of you!
CAPTAIN	No. It's them. It's them that'll be the death of me, if they come and find me still here . . .
JIM	Why? That man – Black Dog – he said they wanted something from you . . .
CAPTAIN	So they do, but they shan't get it, by God! Now listen, both of you. You get me another glass of rum, and I'll tell you. You've both been fair with me. And this lad of yours – I've taken a liking to him. So for his sake, and yours, I'll tell you this, and maybe put you in the way of a lot more than I owe you, or ever could.

130

140

He was a pirate, wasn't he? *The first mention of Flint, the pirate captain, whose evil spirit looms large over the whole story. Although Flint is a fictional buccaneer, there were many real-life pirates in the 18th Century whose deeds inspired as much fear as Flint's. The term buccaneer derives from their practice of stealing cattle from plantations in Spanish America, and drying the meat from them on grills. The French word for these grills is 'boucan'.*

MRS HAWKINS	*(To JIM.)* Bring him his rum.
	(JIM takes the glass, refills it, sets it down. The CAPTAIN drinks, sipping at it this time.)
CAPTAIN	I was one of Flint's men, too, for my sins. His first mate. 150 I was with him when he died. Hot, he was, and trembling, hot as if hell's fire was already roasting him, and his body shrunk to a skeleton. But he gave it to me before he died. Placed it in my hands, and it's in my chest, now, the thing they want, but they'll not take it from me, I'll see that they don't.
MRS HAWKINS	What is it? Money? Gold?
CAPTAIN	Money and gold and a lot more besides. Now, if they should come for me . . . before I've had chance to get away . . . you take that bag of mine . . . take it to that 160 magistrate and be damned to them all . . . but mind they don't catch you first . . . for if they do – they'll show you no mercy . . . they're men that know nothing of human mercy . . .
	(Heavily, he starts to push himself up from his chair.)
MRS HAWKINS	What are you doing . . . ?
CAPTAIN	I've got to go – got to try and get away . . .
MRS HAWKINS	You're going nowhere . . .
CAPTAIN	They'll be coming – I have to go . . .
MRS HAWKINS	Going'll be the death of you . . . 170
CAPTAIN	And staying'll be the death of me as well!
	(He tries to push past MRS HAWKINS, but stumbles again. JIM runs forward and grabs hold of him.)
JIM	Captain . . . !
	(MRS HAWKINS also takes hold of the CAPTAIN and they help him back to his seat. He speaks, rambling, almost incoherent.)

CAPTAIN	I'm done for . . . stay or go there's no difference . . . thought I could escape from him – but there's no escape . . . not from him . . . come back from the grave, he has . . . you see him . . . ? Do you see him there . . . Flint . . . old Flint . . . he's there . . . grinning . . .	180

JIM	*(Shouts.)* There's no one there!

(At the sound of JIM's voice, the CAPTAIN turns to look at him, as if shaken out of a trance. Then, slowly, he lets his head sink down a little and sits forward, heavily.)

MRS HAWKINS	He's sick. And likely to die if we don't do something. We must try and get him to his bed, and then see if we can bring Doctor Livesey. Help me with him.

(Suddenly, offstage, we hear a tapping sound.)

JIM	Listen.	190

(They are still. The tapping sound continues, drawing closer.)

Do you hear that?

MRS HAWKINS	I do. What is it?

(JIM shakes his head. The tapping continues. During the following, the figure of BLIND PEW appears, far to one side of the stage. He's dressed in a ragged cloak, with a hood, has a filthy cloth tied over his eyes, and is finding his way by means of tapping a stick.)

JIM	I'll go and see . . .

MRS HAWKINS	No, Jim . . . !	200

JIM	It's all right. If it is . . . them . . . they won't risk anything while it's still daylight.

Do you see him there? *The Captain's delirium, a mixture of rum and terror, is taking hold of him. But, this incident is one of many with supernatural overtones. Flint's ghost can be said to walk throughout the whole book, wreaking destruction.*

MRS HAWKINS	Just take care . . .

(JIM goes out of the inn through the doorway, as PEW approaches, and calls, softly.)

PEW	Is anyone there? Is their any kind friend to help a poor blind man who lost his sight in the defence of his country? *(He pauses.)* There's someone there. I can feel it. Some kind soul.

JIM	*(Hesitant.)* There is, sir . . .	210

(PEW turns his head sharply towards JIM.)

PEW	A voice – a young voice. *(He shuffles a few steps closer to JIM.)* Tell me, what part of the country is this I'm standing in?

JIM	You're standing outside *The Admiral Benbow* on Black Hill Cove.

PEW	*(Shuffles a few steps closer.)* Then will you give me your hand, young man, and lead me in there?

(JIM hesitates.)

It's a cold afternoon for walking the roads. Your hand.

(He holds out his hand towards JIM. JIM goes to take it. As he   220 *does so, PEW grips his wrist, hard, and twists it round behind his back. JIM cries out. When PEW speaks, now, his voice hisses with vehemence.)*

Now, boy, take me in to the Captain. Take me in straight, or I'll break your arm!

(Gripped by PEW, JIM leads him into the inn. MRS HAWKINS gasps when she sees them.)

MRS HAWKINS	What's this . . . !

PEW	*(Snaps at her.)* Quiet, woman! My business isn't with you. *(Nods towards the CAPTAIN.)* It's with him.	230

(At the sound of PEW's voice, the CAPTAIN stiffens and looks round in terror.)

CAPTAIN	Pew!
PEW	That's right, Bill. Blind Pew it is, and you know why I'm here. *(The CAPTAIN goes to rise.)* Sit where you are! I can't see but I can hear a finger stirring. *(He drops his stick on the floor.)* Business is business, Bill. Hold out your left hand.

(The CAPTAIN holds out his left hand. PEW takes something from his pocket with his right hand, and speaks to JIM.)

PEW   Boy, take his left hand by the wrist and bring it close to my   240
right.

(JIM does so. PEW places something in the CAPTAIN's palm. Then he closes the CAPTAIN's hand round it.)

There, now. It's done. *(He looses JIM.)* Give me my stick!

(JIM picks up PEW's stick and gives it to him. Tapping with the stick, PEW goes out through the doorway, and off. After a short pause, MRS HAWKINS goes to the doorway, watches PEW go, then turns back to the CAPTAIN.)

MRS HAWKINS   What new trouble is this?

(The CAPTAIN opens his palm and looks into it.)   250

CAPTAIN   The Black Spot. That's what it is. My . . . summons. Jim. Take it, will you? Turn it over. Read what it says. My eyes . . . Can't see right . . .

(JIM takes the piece of paper. He turns it over and reads.)

JIM   'You have till dark.'

CAPTAIN   Till dark? There's time, then! We'll do them yet . . . !

(As he speaks, he rises suddenly, but, as he does so, he staggers, stumbles, and falls forward onto the floor. JIM cries out.)

The Black Spot *A summons or judgement given by a pirate crew to a fellow member of the crew who has broken one of their laws. As will be seen later, although they are criminals, the pirates have their own rules and regulations. The Black Spot is Robert Louis Stevenson's own invention.*

JIM	Captain – !

(JIM kneels by the CAPTAIN. MRS HAWKINS runs across, and kneels by him as well. JIM shakes the CAPTAIN by the shoulders.) 260

Captain! Captain!

MRS HAWKINS	Stop it, Jim! Stop! *(She takes JIM by the hands.)* It won't do any good. Nothing will do the poor man good any more. He's dead.

JIM and MRS HAWKINS freeze over the body of the CAPTAIN.

STORYBOARDING Choose four key events from Scene 4, and storyboard them, as if you were making a film. As before, sketch each frame, describe what the audience will hear, and make notes on what the camera is showing.

LANGUAGE Look closely at the way Black Dog speaks. What is there that tells us he is an unpleasant man? What similarities are there between the way Black Dog and the Captain speak?

ARTWORK Make a sketch of the moment when Blind Pew enters, as you think it might appear onstage. Think about what effect you want this moment to have on an audience, and how you would best create this effect for the stage.

CHARACTER STUDY AND HOT-SEATING The Captain dies at the end of this scene. Looking back over this, and the previous scenes, discuss what you know about the Captain.
   Then, in small groups, one of you take on the role of the Captain, and the others question him about his past, why he is in hiding, who or what he seems to be afraid of, and why other characters are pursuing him.

IMPROVISATION It seems clear from the action that, after Black Dog runs from the inn, he goes to Blind Pew, and then Blind Pew makes his way to the inn to give the Captain the Black Spot.
   In twos, create a short scene between Black Dog and Blind Pew, beginning with the moment when Black Dog returns from the inn, and ending with Blind Pew's leaving for the inn.

DISCUSSION In small groups, discuss what you think it is that kills the Captain.

ACT 1 ❖ SCENE 5

ADULT JIM steps forward to narrate. As he does so, MRS HAWKINS goes offstage,
and returns with the CAPTAIN's chest. They try to open it but it's locked

ADULT JIM   I'd never really liked him. And there were times, when, like   1
my mother, I'd wished him gone for the trouble he'd
brought us. But it wasn't only trouble he'd brought. There'd
been a glimpse too of some other world beyond my narrow
horizon . . . A world of open skies and high waves, strong
winds and the taste of salt in the air. A world that called to
me. If I'd known then what horrors I would witness in that
world, perhaps I'd have cursed him as he lay there. But I
didn't, and all I knew was a pity for him – and an
unaccountable feeling of grief, that shook me to the roots   10
of my being.

(MRS HAWKINS has been searching the CAPTAIN for the key to
the chest.)

MRS HAWKINS   Nothing. But he must have the key on him somewhere.

JIM   Perhaps . . . It's round his neck . . .

MRS HAWKINS   You look, then.

(JIM pulls open the CAPTAIN's shirt and sees the key, tied on a
length of string, around his neck. He looks up at his mother.)

JIM   I was right. It's here.

MRS HAWKINS   Give to me. Quickly, now. We must hurry.   20

(JIM takes the key from round the CAPTAIN's neck, gives it to
his mother, and she unlocks the chest. They open it and look
inside, as ADULT JIM narrates.)

ADULT JIM   It was late afternoon, and the sun was sinking. Outside, a
cold wind moaned, and the shadows of the dark crept into
the room.

(MRS HAWKINS takes a leather pouch from the chest and empties it.)

MRS HAWKINS A few coins. Gold and silver, he said. He must've been raving. Still, there's enough here to make up for what he owed.

30

JIM There's something else.

(He reaches inside the chest and takes out a large package, wrapped in oilskin)

A package of some kind.

MRS HAWKINS Take that, as well. I think we'd best be going now.

(They stand, as ADULT JIM narrates.)

ADULT JIM And with the dark came the blind man, and worse horrors.

(Light fades off ADULT JIM as he moves away, leaving the stage very dimly lit. Offstage, we hear the tapping of BLIND PEW's stick.)

40

JIM Listen!

(Pause.)

It's them!

MRS HAWKINS God preserve us, now. Out the back, Jim, and down to the stream. We can hide beneath the bridge until they're gone.

(MRS HAWKINS and JIM exit, on the opposite side of the stage to the doorway. As they go, BLIND PEW enters, on the other side. He gradually makes his way to front centre stage, where he remains still. The CHORUS and PIRATES enter from all sides, keeping towards the back of the stage, so that they remain in shadow, speaking from the darkness.)

50

1st VOICE Night falls.

2nd VOICE Shadows slip from the shadows.

3rd VOICE Thin figures moving along the road.

TREASURE ISLAND
                ACT 1
                SCENE 5

4th VOICE	Footbeats flapping . . .	
5th VOICE	A lantern flashing . . .	
6th VOICE	And voices calling from the rags of the dark.	

(PEW calls out. The PIRATES answer him from the shadows.)

PEW	Down with the door!	60
DIRK	Ay, ay, sir!	
BLACK DOG	All together, lads!	
JACK	One, two, three!	
1st VOICE	The door buckles, splinters . . .	
2nd VOICE	Bursts wide with a crash!	
3rd VOICE	And they're inside . . .	
4th VOICE	Hunting, searching . . .	
5th VOICE	Dogs sniffing the track of their quarry . . .	
6th VOICE	Starved wolves hungry for blood.	

(Once again, PIRATES call from the shadows.)   70

DIRK	Bill's dead!
PEW	Search him! Find his chest!
BLACK DOG	The chest's here! And it's open!
PEW	Anything inside?
JACK	No! It's empty!
PEW	The woman and the boy! Damn and blast them! Out, lads! Scatter and find them! They can't have gone far! Hunt them down! I'll tear out their hearts with my bare hands!

(The CHORUS begin to beat, rhythmically, against the timber, creating the sound of approaching hoofbeats, softly at first,   80
growing louder.)

1st VOICE	Now, in the distance, the sound of thunder . . .
2nd VOICE	A soft thunder, drumming under the ground . . .
3rd VOICE	A storm approaching, though the sky is clear . . .
4th VOICE	It rumbles under the length of the road . . .
5th VOICE	Shivers the earth where his feet stand firm . . .
6th VOICE	Strikes him through with its terrible shockwave.

(The PIRATES call in panic.)

DIRK Horses! They're coming this way!

BLACK DOG Somebody's called the coastguard! 90

JACK It's all up! Run for it, lads!

(PEW calls out in rising terror.)

PEW Dirk? Jack? Black Dog? Where are you? Don't leave me here! You wouldn't leave old Pew! Come back! Help me! Damn and blast you all to hell!

1st VOICE And the storm breaks and the night screams!

2nd VOICE Hoof-thump! Mane-crack!

3rd VOICE The white eyes flashing!

4th VOICE And the earth rears above him!

5th VOICE And tumbles upon him! 100

6th VOICE And splits wide open and swallows him up!

(The drumming grows louder, as PEW raises his arms above his head for protection and screams. Then it stops, abruptly.)

(Silence and blackout.)

---

the coastguard *The job of the coastguard was to guard the coast against invasion by a foreign enemy (a very real threat in the 18th Century), and lawbreakers such as smugglers and pirates.*

DISCUSSION AND WRITING As a class, discuss why you think it is the playwright has chosen to show Blind Pew's death in the way he has. Then, imagine you are directing this scene, and describe how you would stage it. Think about what effect you want it to have on the audience, and how you might best achieve that effect in the theatre.

ACTING In the play you don't find out who sent for the coastguard.

In small groups, discuss who you think called them, and why. Create a short scene showing how the coastguard was sent for.

DISCUSSION AND ARTWORK In small groups, discuss how you would shoot Scene 5 if you were making a film. Then, in pairs, choose four moments from the scene and storyboard them. Compare these ideas with the ideas from above.

As a class, use these ideas to discuss the differences between staging a scene for the theatre, and shooting a scene for a film.

WRITING Imagine you are either Jim or Mrs Hawkins, hiding beneath the bridge and watching as the pirates break into the inn.

Write down, as a monologue or poem, all that you are thinking and feeling at the time. Compare your work with others and discuss the differences.

CHARACTER STUDY Begin to compile a study of all the main characters who appear in the play. List all the main characters who have appeared in this act, make notes on what you know of them so far, and what part they have played in the action of the story.

Some will not appear again, and some will continue through the rest of the play. You might add to your notes as you read on.

THE VOYAGE
ACT 2 ❖ SCENE 1

ADULT JIM enters alone and speaks to the audience.

ADULT JIM   The blind man was dead, ridden down beneath the hooves   1
of the coastguards' horses. The rest of the gang were
scattered, escaped. With the body of the Captain still lying
where it had fallen, neither my mother nor myself had any
desire to return to the inn. So it seemed the only thing to
be done was for us to make our way to the house of Squire
Trelawney, where he was dining with Doctor Livesey, to tell
them our story, and to discover just what it was that had
brought two men to their deaths – and was destined to
bring death to many more.   10

*(SQUIRE TRELAWNEY, DOCTOR LIVESEY, MRS HAWKINS,
JIM, and HUNTER enter. JIM carries the package he took from
the CAPTAIN's body. They gather around a table, centre, as they
speak. HUNTER stands a little further off.)*

TRELAWNEY   Money! What else would those villains be after but money?
What do they care about but money? I'll warrant that what
Jim has here is some clue to the finding of Flint's treasure!

LIVESEY   You've heard of this Flint?

TRELAWNEY   Heard of him? Why, man, he was the bloodiest buccaneer
that sailed the high seas. Blackbeard was a child compared   20
to Flint. If half the stories they tell of him were true, he was
more devil than man.

Squire Trelawney *A squire was a country gentleman and chief landowner
in a district — and therefore the most important man.*

Blackbeard *Edward Teach, a famous and feared real-life pirate.*

MRS HAWKINS	That's just what the Captain called him, wasn't it, Jim? A devil. He seemed afraid of him, even though he was dead. As if he feared somehow perhaps he wasn't.
TRELAWNEY	I can imagine it! His crew had reason to fear Flint almost as much as those he robbed and murdered. A cold-hearted, blood-hungry killer was Flint. A monster! But, if the stories are true, a mighty rich monster. And the whereabouts of those riches have never been discovered. Except, perhaps, till now.

30

LIVESEY	Then we wait on Jim to reveal the truth of it. Let us see the package.

(ADULT JIM narrates as child JIM takes the package out of his coat.)

ADULT JIM	I remember the heaviness of it, its weight in my hands, heavier than it should have been for its size. And I remember too the looks on their faces, as they watched, their eyes fixed on me, shining . . .

(JIM offers the package to the DOCTOR.)

40

JIM	Doctor . . .
TRELAWNEY	I'll take it.

(The SQUIRE takes the package off JIM.)

Oilskin. And sewn all around the edges. *(To HUNTER.)* Hunter. Your knife, please.

HUNTER	Yes, sir.

(HUNTER comes forward and gives a small knife to the SQUIRE.)

TRELAWNEY	Now. Go and lock the door.
HUNTER	Sir.

50

(HUNTER goes and locks the door.)

LIVESEY	*(Objecting.)* Come, Trelawney . . .

TRELAWNEY	Come, Livesey. Two men that we know of have lost their lives for this. We cannot be too cautious.
	(TRELAWNEY carefully slits open the package with the knife. He takes out a piece of folded parchment.)
	Parchment! Damn me if this isn't a map!
LIVESEY	Unfold it, and we'll see.
	(TRELAWNEY unfolds the parchment, and spreads it out on the table.)
MRS HAWKINS	You were right, sir!
TRELAWNEY	I knew it! Pardon me, Mrs Hawkins, but damn me again if I wasn't! Hunter. Bring us the lamp.
	(HUNTER brings a lamp and joins the group, holding the lamp over the map. All bend over the map and gaze down. ADULT JIM narrates)
ADULT JIM	And I see it now as I saw it then, for the first time, lit by the glow of the lamp, and I see our faces lit too in the flickering shadow, as we gazed down in wonder at what lay spread out before us.

60

TRELAWNEY	An island!	70
JIM	It's shaped like a dragon.	
LIVESEY	Nine miles long, five across.	
TRELAWNEY	With lines of latitude and longitude . . .	
HUNTER	Hills and bays and rivers all marked . . .	
JIM	Spy-Hill, White Rock, North Inlet . . .	
MRS HAWKINS	This writing here. What does it say?	

(ADULT JIM speaks what's written there, as if recalling the words by heart)

ADULT JIM 'The bar silver is in the north cache; the arms are easy found. Tall tree, Spy-Glass shoulder, bearing to a point to the North of Nor-Nor-East. Bulk of treasure here.' 80

(TRELAWNEY cries out.)

TRELAWNEY Bulk of treasure here! We have it! This is it, the very thing! Flint's treasure map! And before long we shall have the treasure itself!

(He breaks from the group, walks up and down excitedly.0

Livesey! You will give up your practice at once! Tomorrow, I start for Bristol to find us a ship. In three weeks – two weeks – ten days! In ten days' time we'll have the best ship and the choicest crew in England. You'll be ship's doctor. 90
I shall be Admiral, of course . . .

LIVESEY Of course.

TRELAWNEY And we'll take Hunter . . .

An island *See the map on page v. Although its location isn't given in the book, it is supposed to be somewhere in the Caribbean.*

Bristol *The nearest large port.*

35

HUNTER	Me, sir?
TRELAWNEY	Yes! You, sir! And Jim! We mustn't forget Jim! Jim shall come as cabin boy!
LIVESEY	With his mother's permission.
TRELAWNEY	Oh, yes. Certainly. Mrs Hawkins. What do you say to your boy coming with us?
MRS HAWKINS	He's more than a boy, sir. It's up to him. If he wishes to go, I won't speak against it. *(To JIM.)* Do you want to go, Jim?
JIM	Yes, Mother. I do.
TRELAWNEY	Good! It's settled then . . .
LIVESEY	Trelawney. I will go with you, once I have found a replacement for my practice here. But I must say this. We are not the only ones who know of the map. Those that attacked the inn tonight will not be far off. We must none of us go alone until we get to sea. Jim especially will need protection . . .
TRELAWNEY	You're right. Hunter shall stay by him until it's time to leave.
HUNTER	I'll be glad to, sir.
LIVESEY	And none of us must breathe a word about what it is we've found, or our destination.
TRELAWNEY	You're in the right of it again, Livesey. I swear to you, sir, that I for one shall be as silent as the grave.
LIVESEY	And we all swear the same.
	(The others nod their agreement.)
TRELAWNEY	Come, then. We must prepare for our journey. We shall have fair winds, a quick passage, an easy landing – and then – treasure! We'll dig up and bring back enough gold and silver for us all to roll in ever after!

100

110

120

(TRELAWNEY picks up the map, preparing to leave. LIVESEY holds his hand out and, after a moment's pause, gives the map to LIVESEY. JIM's mother, LIVESEY, HUNTER and TRELAWNEY go, leaving JIM and ADULT JIM onstage.)

ACTING Act 2 begins with Jim and his mother already with the Squire and the Doctor, and about to open the Captain's package.
In small groups, create the scene that comes just before this, when Jim and his mother arrive at the Squire's House, to tell him and the Doctor about what has happened.

FREEZE FRAMING Create a freeze-frame of the moment when the Squire opens the package and the map is seen for the first time. Let each character speak their thoughts and feelings as they see the map.
You could also sketch this as a storyboard, writing the characters' thoughts in thought-bubbles, or captions.

CHARACTER STUDY As a class, discuss the differences in character between Doctor Livesey and Squire Trelawney. Support your ideas with examples of how the two characters speak, and what they say.

WRITING Imagine you're Hunter. Write a letter from him to a friend, or relation, in which you explain that you're going away, and why. Put down your thoughts and feelings about the situation in the letter.

ACT 2 ❖ SCENE 2

ADULT JIM narrates.

ADULT JIM   In the weeks that followed, as I waited for news of our
leaving, my imagination was filled with thoughts of that
island – its bright shores washed by the white waves, forests
green and deep and rich, the shining peaks of its hills – the
whole place a shimmering jewel, filled with sweet voices
that rose on the wind and called to me, promising
adventure and escape. And I thought the day would never
come when I would hear word of my departure. But at last,
it did.

(JIM's mother enters, with HUNTER behind her.)   1

MRS HAWKINS   Jim.

(JIM turns to her.)

Mr Hunter's brought a letter from Squire Trelawney. He's
found a ship at last.

*(HUNTER steps forward and gives the letter to JIM. JIM reads it.
As he does so, TRELAWNEY enters, to one side, and speaks the
contents of the letter.)*

TRELAWNEY   She lies at anchor, ready for sea, and you never imagined a
sweeter vessel. A child might sail her. Two hundred tons.
Name – the *Hispaniola*.   2

(TRELAWNEY goes. JIM gives the letter back to HUNTER.)

JIM   It's time to leave, then?

The *Hispaniola* But what kind of ship is she? In the book she's described
as a schooner – a rigged ship with more than one mast. It was an
average-sized ship, built for speed.

MRS HAWKINS	Yes.
JIM	When?
HUNTER	We're to take the coach to Bristol tomorrow morning.

(MRS HAWKINS goes to the side of the stage, picks up a small travelling bag from there, and takes it to JIM, as ADULT JIM narrates.)

ADULT JIM And the next morning came, and I stood at the door of *The Admiral Benbow*, above the cove where I'd lived since I was 30 born. A fine, warm, August morning, it was, the sky blue, and the sea washing over the rocks below.

(JIM takes the bag from his MRS HAWKINS.)

MRS HAWKINS	Goodbye, then, Jim.
JIM	Goodbye, Mrs Hawkins.
MRS HAWKINS	Look after yourself.
JIM	I will. But what about you? Will you be all right while I'm gone?

MRS HAWKINS Don't fear for me. I shall get on here well enough. You see that you do all the Squire and the Doctor tell you . . . and 40 bear yourself well . . . and make me proud to have you as my son . . .

JIM I will. I promise. And I'll return before you know it – with my pockets filled with treasure! Gold and silver! Diamonds and rubies and sapphires! So much I'll hardly be able to walk for the weight of it all!

MRS HAWKINS You say so, do you?

JIM I know so! And then, you'll be able to sell this place, and live like a lady, and never have to wait on others again.

MRS HAWKINS Then the quicker you're gone, the quicker these things may 50 come about. Go on, now. It's time.

(JIM turns to go. He turns back, and he and his mother embrace. He turns and moves offstage, with HUNTER. His mother watches him go)

ADULT JIM   And I turned from her, and stepped down the road, and turned the corner, away from my home, down towards the village where the coach was waiting to take me to Bristol.

(JIM and HUNTER have gone. MRS HAWKINS turns and walks offstage, in the opposite direction.)

DISCUSSION As a class, discuss what you think it is that attracts Jim to the idea of sailing for buried treasure. What are his motives?

HOT-SEATING In small groups, one takes on the role of Mrs Hawkins, and the others question her about all that has happened so far.
● How does she feel about her son going away on the voyage?
● What are her chief fears and concerns?
● Does she completely trust both the Doctor and the Squire with Jim's welfare?

WRITING Using ideas from the above activity, imagine you're Mrs Hawkins, watching your son walk away down the road to get the coach for Bristol. Write down your immediate thoughts and feelings, as a monologue in prose or poetry.

ACT 2 ❖ SCENE 3

CHORUS enter, as SAILORS, brisk, lively, creating the impression of a busy, bustling sea-port.

1st SAILOR   And he arrives there late next morning . . .   1

2nd SAILOR   Steps down, still sleepy, from the long night's coach ride . . .

3rd SAILOR   Into the salt-sharp, sea-bright, ocean port . . .

4th SAILOR   Where tall ships jostle the crowded harbour . . .

5th SAILOR   Masts sway . . .

6th SAILOR   Sails slap . . .

1st SAILOR   Ropes strain at their moorings . . .

2nd SAILOR   Eager to break loose . . .

3rd SAILOR   Leave dry land behind . . .

4th SAILOR   Sailing for foreign shores, distant horizons . . .   10

5th SAILOR   And where the songs of the sailors lift to the breeze . . .

6th SAILOR   And circle the sun with the wheeling gulls.

(The CHORUS sings a sea-shanty. JIM and HUNTER enter, JIM carrying his bag, and gazing around him in wonder. When the sea-shanty is finished, TRELAWNEY enters to JIM and greets him heartily. We are in the room TRELAWNEY has taken at an inn on the harbour-side.)

TRELAWNEY   Jim! A pleasure to see you again! Good journey? Capital!
(To HUNTER.) Hunter. Take Jim's bag, stow it on board.
(To JIM.) You'll go on board yourself later, my boy.   20

A sea-shanty *A sailors' song, often used to accompany heavy work on deck, such as raising the anchor or hoisting the sails. Sea-shanties often told the stories of noteable events at sea, such as battles or storms or shipwrecks.*

(HUNTER takes
JIM'S bag and goes.
TRELAWNEY
continues speaking
hurriedly, hardly
pausing for breath
or allowing any
interruption.)

For now, here's
your first
command. Go to
the *Spyglass Inn*.
It's just along the
harbour. You can't
miss it. Introduce
yourself to the
landlord. He's to
be our ship's cook.

30

Capital fellow! A real sea-dog. Lost his leg fighting for King
and country and he's eager to take ship again. I met him by
chance and it was a fortune that I did. He's assembled the
best crew you could find. I think he must know half the
seafaring men in Bristol. You tell him that he's to come
immediately. For we sail tomorrow, Jim. Tomorrow, with
the rising of the sun!

40

JIM	Did you say he'd lost a leg, sir?
TRELAWNEY	That's right. What of it? Doesn't scare you, does it?
JIM	No, sir . . . only the Captain, when he first came to our inn . . . he warned me to look out for a man with one leg . . . a seafaring man . . .
TRELAWNEY	Did he, now? And you think my man and his might be the same?
JIM	I don't know. It just . . . put me in mind of his warning . . .

50

TRELAWNEY	Then put it clean out of your mind! I'm a fair judge of character, and I say our cook's no more a villain than I am. I'll stake my reputation and my life on it! You get along, now and make your acquaintance with him. You'll see straight away I'm right.

(TRELAWNEY turns from JIM.)

JIM Squire – you haven't told me the gentleman's name . . . 60

(SILVER enters, his left leg cut off at the knee, supporting himself with a crutch.)

SILVER Silver. John Silver. Long John, some call me.

(JIM turns to SILVER. TRELAWNEY goes. We are now at SILVER's inn. The chorus of SAILORS gathers, as if at the inn. Others enter and join them – including, TOM MORGAN, GEORGE MERRY, and SILVER's wife, REBECCA. BLACK DOG is also among them.)

Such is my name, to be sure. And what might yours be?

JIM My name's Jim, Mr Silver. Jim Hawkins. Squire Trelawney 70
sent me . . .

SILVER The Squire! Then you must be our cabin-boy. Give me your hand, Jim. *(He shakes JIM's hand.)* Rebecca! Come over here. Meet Jim Hawkins, cabin-boy on the *Hispaniola*. This is my missus, Jim. Rebecca Silver.

JIM Pleased to meet you, Mrs Silver.

REBECCA Likewise, Jim.

SILVER He has some news from the Squire. We have our sailing orders, I'll be bound.

JIM That's right, Mr Silver. The Squire says you're to come 80
straight away. We sail tomorrow.

SILVER Tomorrow! And not a day too soon! You'll be looking forward to it, eh? A young lad out on his first sea-voyage.

I remember the first time I went to sea. About the same age as you, I was. He's a fine-looking, lad, don't you think, Rebecca?

REBECCA   He is, that. The kind of boy we might have been blessed with John, had the powers that be granted it so.

SILVER   The very thought was in my own mind. I wish I was young again, Jim. No more than a lad, like you, and all the world   90
before me.

(During the above, JIM, has been looking around at the SAILORS, and his eyes have suddenly fallen upon BLACK DOG. He gives a gasp of recognition. At the same time, BLACK DOG sees JIM.)

JIM   That man . . . !

SILVER   Eh? What is it?

JIM   That man there! It's Black Dog!

(BLACK DOG jumps up.)

REBECCA   I don't care who he is! He's trying to make off without   100
paying his score!

SILVER   George! After him!

JIM   Stop him!

(BLACK DOG runs off, pushing his way past several SAILORS, and GEORGE MERRY chases after him.)

REBECCA   What did you say his name was?

JIM   Black Dog – he's a buccaneer – one of those who attacked our inn.

SILVER   The Squire told me of that. One of those swabs, was he.

    paying his score *Paying for what he's had.*

And in my house! Tom Morgan! Was that you drinking   110
with him?

(MORGAN comes across to SILVER.)

MORGAN   Yes, John . . .

SILVER   You never clapped eyes on him before, did you?

MORGAN   No, sir. Never.

REBECCA   That's good for. If I knowed you was mixed up with the like
of that scum, you'd never have put another foot in this
house!

SILVER   Get back to your place, for a lubber, Tom Morgan.

(MORGAN returns to his place.)   130

REBECCA   He's an honest man, Tom Morgan. Only he's stupid.

SILVER   Not you, though, Jim. You're a smart lad, I can see that.
Smart as paint. Tell me that swab's name again?

JIM   Black Dog.

SILVER   Black Dog. I don't know the name. Do you, Rebecca?

REBECCA   No. But now I come to think of it, I do recall seeing him in
here before – only once or twice. And both times he was
with a blind beggar . . .

JIM   Yes! That was another of them! Blind Pew!

REBECCA   Pew. Aye, that was his name. He looked a shark, he did,   140
John. And to think the two of them were here, drinking our
rum, and we never knowed what they was.

(GEORGE MERRY enters.)

MERRY   I lost him, John.

SILVER   Lost him, did you, George! That's bad. And him never
having paid his score, neither!

REBECCA   It's a bad business all round. There's only one thing for it,

John. You and the boy here had best go straight away and tell the Squire all about it.

SILVER   You're right, Rebecca. Dooty is dooty, and the Squire must be told. Even though it might be he thinks twice about having me aboard, now, knowing I keep such bad company.   150

(SQUIRE TRELAWNEY and DOCTOR LIVESEY enter to JIM and SILVER. REBECCA, the chorus of SAILORS go. We have now returned to TRELAWNEY's room.)

TRELAWNEY   Nonsense! I won't hear of it! You weren't to know who the scoundrel was. And it shows an honest heart that you came and told us of it straight away.

SILVER   I'm mighty relieved to hear you say that, sir. For the sake of my honour and trust more than anything.   150

TRELAWNY   Your honour's beyond doubt, Silver! And you have our complete trust. Isn't that so, Livesey?

LIVESEY   Indeed he does.

SILVER   Thank you very much, gentlemen. I am greatly obliged to you. I'll take my leave of you, now. You have business to attend to, and so do I. *(To JIM.)* I'll see you later, boy, once we're aboard.

(SILVER turns and makes his way off. TRELAWNEY calls after him.)

TRELAWNEY   All hands aboard by four this afternoon.   160

(SILVER turns and salutes TRELAWNEY with great ceremony.)

SILVER   Aye, aye, sir.

(He grins, then turns and goes. TRELAWNEY turns to LIVESEY and JIM.)

TRELAWNEY   What did I tell you? The man's a perfect card!

LIVESEY   I have to say, Trelawney, I agree with you. You have made a good choice there. John Silver certainly suits me.

ACT 2 ❖ SCENE 4

HUNTER enters. During this scene, JIM moves away to sit a little apart. He takes a piece of rope, and practises tying a ship's knot, constantly failing, and trying again.

HUNTER	Begging your pardon, Squire . . .	1
TRELAWNEY	Yes, Hunter. What is it?	
HUNTER	Captain Smollett is here, sir. He wishes to speak with you.	
TRELAWNEY	Show him in, then.	
HUNTER	Very good, sir.	
	(HUNTER goes. TRELAWNEY turns to JIM.)	
TRELAWNEY	I wonder what he wants. He's an able man, by all accounts, but stiff, Livesey. Stiff! There's something in him that makes me bristle.	
	(CAPTAIN SMOLLETT enters.)	10
TRELAWNEY	Captain Smollett! All's well I hope? Everything shipshape and seaworthy?	
SMOLLETT	I'll speak to you plain, sir, and what I have to say is this. I don't like this voyage and I don't like the men.	
TRELAWNEY	Don't you, indeed! And perhaps you don't like the ship, either!	
SMOLLETT	She seems a good enough craft . . .	
TRELAWNEY	Or your employer, eh? Perhaps you don't like him . . . !	
	(LIVESEY cuts in.)	
LIVESEY	Captain. You have either said too much or not enough. You say you don't like this voyage? Now, why?	20
SMOLLETT	When I was engaged, I was given to understand that neither I nor any of the crew were to know our destination	

47

until we had set sail. So far so good. I've sailed under sealed orders before. But now I find that every man before mast knows more than I do!

LIVESEY Indeed? And what do they know?

SMOLLETT That we're sailing for treasure – and that you have a map of our destination. And what's more, the very latitude and longitude of it are common knowledge! 30

LIVESEY Trelawney. How do you explain this?

TRELAWNEY I can't!

LIVESEY We all swore to keep the matter secret!

TRELAWNEY I never breathed a word of it, Livesey!

LIVESEY Then who did? Perhaps it was me, or Jim, here, or Hunter . . .

SMOLLETT It doesn't much matter who it was. What matters is, the secret's out. And what are we to do about it?

LIVESEY What do you suggest, Captain?

SMOLLETT Going after treasure's a troublesome business. But, if you are 40 determined to proceed with this voyage . . .

TRELAWNEY We are.

SMOLLETT Then I feel it only wise to take certain precautions.

LIVESEY Which are?

SMOLLETT First, whoever has this map in his possession, let him keep it to himself, and let no more be spoken of it, or of treasure, among the men. There's been too much loose talk already.

---

sealed orders *Secret orders, not to be opened until the ship has put to sea.*

every man before mast *'before the mast' – the sailors' quarters were generally forward of the mast whereas the gentlemen, captain, etc. were berthed aft of the mast.*

LIVESEY	*(Looking at TRELAWNEY.)* Indeed there has. And next?
SMOLLETT	The powder and arms. They're being stored in the fore-hold. I suggest it might be better to store them in the hold beneath your own cabin. And give all your own people berths in the same quarter.
LIVESEY	So that the stern of the ship becomes a garrison, with all weapons to hand.
SMOLLETT	You have my drift exactly, Doctor.
LIVESEY	And then if trouble does arise . . .
SMOLLETT	Not that I believe it will. If I did I wouldn't set sail. But I am the ship's captain, and responsible for the life of every man aboard of her. I'd be failing in my duty if I didn't ensure that every precaution against trouble had been taken.
LIVESEY	And so it shall be, Captain Smollett, just as you say. You can rest assured of that. Can't he, Trelawney?
TRELAWNEY	*(Sullenly.)* Yes.
SMOLLETT	Very good. In that case, I'll take my leave of you and go aboard. Gentlemen.
	(SMOLLETT goes.)
TRELAWNEY	That man is intolerable! Did you hear him, Livesey? He more or less accused me of loose talk! Me! His employer! I've half a mind to go after him and . . .
LIVESEY	You'll do no such thing. The man talked sense. The most sense I've heard since this enterprise was begun. And you're to be congratulated for it.
TRELAWNEY	What?

50

60

70

fore-hold *The holds were the spaces beneath the decks where goods and provisions were stored, and covered by hatches. The fore is the front of the ship. So, the fore-hold is the hold at the front of the ship.*

LIVESEY   Contrary to all my notions, I believe you've managed to get two honest men aboard – that man, and John Silver!

(TRELAWNEY and LIVESEY go, leaving JIM alone still working at tying the knot.)

ARTWORK When Jim arrives in Bristol, he's thrilled and excited. Create four frames for a storyboard of a film, showing what he sees and hears on his arrival, that would create this sense of thrill and excitement.

DISCUSS Jim is at first suspicious of Silver when he hears that he has only one leg, but Squire Trelawney dismisses his suspicion.
    As a class, discuss what else happens in the scene to persuade Jim he has nothing to fear from Silver.

DISCUSSION AND WRITING Although, in this scene, Silver tries to put himself across as an honest man, there are several clues in this scene which point towards the later discovery that he is a pirate. In small groups, discuss what evidence you can find in the text for this, then make a note of all the clues you can find that he is, in fact, a pirate.

ACTING In small groups, discuss how you think Squire Trelawney first becomes acquainted with Silver. Then, using these ideas, create a short scene showing the first meeting between Trelawney and Silver. Other characters, such as Doctor Livesey, George Merry, and Rebecca Silver, may also appear in the scene.

DISCUSSION As a class, discuss how you think it is that the crew came to know about the purpose of the voyage. Who do you think let the secret out, and how?

HOT-SEATING In small groups, try these three activities:

1 One takes on the role of Captain Smollett, and the others question him about what he thinks and feels about the voyage, why he's concerned, and what he thinks about other characters, such as Squire Trelawney, Doctor Livesey, Jim, and Silver.

2 One takes on the role of Squire Trelawney, and the others question him about what he thinks of Captain Smollett and his attitude.

3 One takes on the role of Doctor Livesey, and the others question him about what he thinks of Captain Smollett, and the Squire, and Silver.

ACT 2 ❖ SCENE 5

ADULT JIM narrates.

ADULT JIM   A troublesome business. A dangerous business. But how   1
little I knew it, then. How little I knew of the human soul,
and what gold can do to it. For what lay ahead was no
voyage of childish adventure, no innocent isle of treasure. It
was a country of betrayals, bloodshed and horror, filled
with the darkness of the human heart.

(SILVER enters.)

SILVER   What's all this talk of darkness? Horror and bloodshed?
Those are no thoughts to fill a lad's head with. It's the light
we're sailing into, Jim. The golden light of the sun, burning   10
high and bright in a hot blue sky! Light in our eyes and
laughter in our hearts, and a life filled up with joy to
overflowing. That's the treasure we're after.

(JIM has succeeded in tying the knot. He shows it to SILVER.)

JIM   Done it! Look!

SILVER   A sheepshank! Couldn't've tied one better myself. You're
smart, Jim. Smart as paint. I knew it the minute I clapped
eyes on you. And we'll have you a regular seafaring man
before we're out of harbour!

SILVER claps his arm round JIM's shoulders, and the two of   20
them make their way up on to a raised area. ADULT JIM
remains below.

ADULT JIM   So he wooed me with his words, spun a web of fine gold

sheepshank *A particular type of knot. Several types of knots served a*
variety of purposes on board sailing ships, and all sailors had to master the
tying of them.

about me, as we stood on deck in the dawn light, watching
the sun clear the far horizon, and the ship sprang to life
about me, and I caught my breath in the sharp salt wind.

*(Chorus of SAILORS enters, with GEORGE MERRY, ISRAEL
HANDS, REDCAP, TOM MORGAN, CAPTAIN SMOLLETT,
LIVESEY, TRELAWNEY, and HUNTER. Also another sailor,
DICK. All SAILORS create the impression of a ship. CHORUS
and others narrate.)*

1st SAILOR	Dawn comes and the night's work's done.
MERRY	Everything stowed, fastened, battened.
2nd SAILOR	The ship's company piped aboard.
REDCAP	Farwells made, orders given.
SMOLLETT	All hands on deck! Jump to it man!
3rd SAILOR	And our mooring's are loosed and the anchor's weighed!
HANDS	Tip us a stave, Barbecue!
SILVER	That I will, Israel!

*(SILVER sings out the verse of the shanty, as some of the
SAILORS mime turning the capstan.)*

SILVER	Fifteen men on a dead man's chest
ALL	Yo! Ho! Ho! And a bottle of rum!

---

piped aboard *Signals and commands were often given by the boatswain
(pronounced bo'sun) on a special whistle. Once all the crew had come
aboard, the boatswain gave such a signal to the captain to let him know
that all was ready for sailing.*

anchor's weighed *To weigh the anchor means to raise the anchor.*

tip us a stave *Slang seamen's term for 'sing us a song'.*

capstan *A thick, revolving wooden cylinder around which the ship's cable
was wound by means of wooden poles in order to raise the anchor.*

SILVER	Drink and the devil had done for the rest.	
ALL	Yo! Ho! Ho! And a bottle of rum!	
SILVER	We hit a storm in 'forty-seven	
ALL	Yo! Ho! Ho! And a bottle of rum!	
SILVER	And many a man was sent to heaven	
ALL	Yo! Ho! Ho! And a bottle of rum!	
SILVER	The rope, the rum and the Yellow Jack	50
ALL	Yo! Ho! Ho! And a bottle of rum!	
SILVER	Delivered the rest to hell and back.	
ALL	Yo! Ho! Ho! And a bottle of rum!	
SILVER	But one man of her crew alive	
ALL	Yo! Ho! Ho! And a bottle of rum!	
SILVER	That put to sea with seventy-five	
ALL	Yo! Ho! Ho! And a bottle of rum!	
	(JOHN stops singing. The men cheer.)	
4th SAILOR	The anchor's a-weigh, and the ship casts free . . .	
MORGAN	Loose of her moorings, out from the harbour . . .	60
DICK	And the land slips away and we turn to the south . . .	
5th SAILOR	As we hoist the sails . . .	
HANDS	And they fill with the wind . . .	
6th SAILOR	And it drives us onward across the world.	

LANGUAGE Adult Jim says of Silver: *So he wooed me with his words . . .*

More than any other character in the play, Silver uses language in a lively, colourful, sometimes almost poetic way. And he uses it for different purposes: to charm, excite, deceive, or just tell a good story. He is, in many ways, a complete master of spoken language.

Make a list, from this and previous scenes, of all the words and phrases used by Silver, that you find particularly colourful, attractive or powerful – words and phrases that show him as a 'master of language'. You can add to this list as you read on through the play.

WRITING As Jim, write a last letter home to your mother just before you set sail. Tell her all you've seen and heard, all that has happened, how you feel, what you hope will happen, what you're looking forward to.

Remember that, at this point in time, you like and admire Silver. Also, you want to allay any fears and worries she still might have.

DISCUSSION In this scene, Silver speaks directly to Adult Jim. In 'real' terms, this can't happen, because Adult Jim is the narrator, looking back on the past, and Silver is a figure from his past. But Silver steps out of the past and speaks to him. This is a 'non-naturalistic' use of theatre – in other words, it's something that couldn't actually happen in real life.

As a class, discuss why you think the playwright has written this section, and what point or effect you think he's trying to make by having Silver step out of the action and speak to Adult Jim. Are there any other 'non-naturalistic' moments in the previous scenes in the play?

ARTWORK Imagine you're staging this play. Make a sketch of your stage design to show how you would create the ship, or the effect of the ship, onstage. Show what props and pieces of scenery you would use, what activities you'd have going on, and where, and where characters would be standing. And remember, the ship must be able to be created quickly.

ACT 2 ❖ SCENE 6

TRELAWNEY, LIVESEY, HUNTER and SMOLLETT go. SAILORS and the rest go
about their duties. SILVER stands next to JIM and they gaze outwards together.

SILVER   There's nothing like, Jim. Casting off from land, with a full   1
wind in your sails. The sky above you and the waves
beneath, and nothing but a few planks of timber and sheets
of canvas between you and eternity. It makes my heart sing,
it does. It sounds the very depths of me. The sea's a great
mystery, lad, a mystery that calls to every one of us born.
And who can fathom it, eh? Not I, though I've sailed it
these forty years.

(He pats JIM on the shoulder, and goes. JIM remains, looking out
to sea. ADULT JIM narrates from below.)   10

ADULT JIM   There's little to tell of the journey. I was set to work,
helping Silver in the galley. And unwearyingly kind to me,
he was, and patient, with always a cheering word or a tale
of his times at sea. And I saw, too, how respected he was by
the rest of the men, how in all things they deferred to him,
as if he was their true captain.

(HANDS speaks to JIM.)

HANDS   He's no common man, is Long John. He had good
schooling in his younger days, and can speak like a book
when he's minded.   20

MERRY   And brave, too. A lion's nothing alongside of Barbecue.

JIM   Why do you call him Barbecue?

---

 galley *The place on board ship where the food is cooked.*

HANDS	He's ship's cook, isn't he? There's no man alive more skilled than he at skewering fresh meat on the end of a spike.
	(MORGAN, MERRY and REDCAP all laugh at this. SILVER has entered. He speaks sharply to them.)
SILVER	That's enough of that idle talk, Israel Hands! Be about your duties. And the rest of you. Or it'll be nothing but ship's biscuits you'll get to crack your teeth on. *(To JIM.)* You come along with me, now, Jim. There's work to be done, if these lubbers are going to have anything to fill their bellies
	(SILVER and JIM go. ADULT JIM narrates as CAPTAIN SMOLLETT, TRELAWNEY and LIVESEY enter.)
ADULT JIM	On the whole, it was a happy voyage, and every man on board well content – except for the Captain and the Squire. The Squire made no bones about the matter – he despised the Captain. And the Captain, on his part, remained stiff and distant, and never spoke, but when spoken to.
TRELAWNEY	Well, Captain. What have you to say about the men now? A fine crew, are they not?
SMOLLETT	I'll own I seem to have been wrong about them. There's some of them as brisk as I'd like to see.
TRELAWNEY	And the ship?
SMOLLETT	She's a good ship.
	(TRELAWNEY turns to LIVESEY.)
TRELAWNEY	There, Livesey . . .
SMOLLETT	But we haven't reached our destination. And we're not home yet. And I say again, I don't like this voyage!

30

40

---

 ship's biscuits *A kind of biscuit given to seamen as a staple diet, and well-famed for their extreme hardness.*

(SMOLLETT turns briskly from TRELAWNEY and goes. TRELAWNEY speaks in a fury.) | 50

TRELAWNEY Confound the man, Livesey! A trifle more of him and I shall explode!

(TRELAWNEY marches off, angrily. SILVER enters with JIM. JIM is carrying a large stone bottle. SILVER speaks to LIVESEY.) | 60

SILVER Begging your pardon, Doctor. It's grog time for the men, and I was wondering if you might be partial to a cup yourself.

LIVESEY Very decent of you, Silver. Yes, I will take a little. | 70

SILVER George Merry. Give the good Doctor a cup. Be sharp about it!

(MERRY gets a cup and gives it to LIVESEY.)

Fill the Doctor's cup for him, Jim, then see to these others.

LIVESEY Don't fill it, Jim. Just a little, if you please.

(JIM pours some of the rum into the DOCTOR's cup, then fills cups for some of the other men. LIVESEY drinks, and gasps. SILVER grins.)

SILVER What do you say, Doctor? A fine drop of grog, isn't it?

(LIVESEY speaks, his voice hoarse.)   80

LIVESEY   Yes, Silver. Very fine indeed.

SILVER   Will you take a drop more?

LIVESEY   No . . . ! No thank you, Silver. One drop will be . . . quite
                sufficent . . . thank you.

                (He gives the cup back to MERRY, who drains what LIVESEY
                has left. Still reeling from the effects of the rum LIVESEY goes.
                SILVER turns to JIM.)

SILVER   Have you done, Jim?

JIM   Yes, Mr Silver.

SILVER   Let's take a little ease, then. Sit you down alongside me   90
                here, and have a yarn with Long John.

                (SILVER and JIM sit together, away from the others. As they sit,
                ADULT JIM narrates.)

ADULT JIM   So we drove on through fair weather, south by south-west,
                with a steady breeze and a quiet sea. And during those
                warm and sunlit days, it was my greatest pleasure to be in
                his company and listen, entranced, to the many fantastic
                tales he told.

SILVER   It's a great pity I don't have Cap'n Flint with me on this
                voyage.   100

JIM   Captain Flint? The pirate?

SILVER   No, not him. This Cap'n Flint I'm talking of, she's a parrot.
                I had her with me on most my voyages, before I was
                dismasted. And I'd've brought her with me on this, only
                she's too old now.

before I was dismasted *Literally, to dismast a ship was to break off one of
its masts. But here, Silver is referring to the loss of his leg.*

JIM	How old is she?
SILVER	Two hundred years, maybe. And don't you be surprised at that, for they lives forever, mostly, do those birds. Before I had her, she sailed along the Spanish Main with Captain England, the pirate.

110

JIM	She must have seen some wickedness in her life, then.
SILVER	She has, Jim, it's true. If anybody's seen more wickedness in the world than that bird, it can only be the Devil himself. She's smelled powder, sure enough. And you should hear her squawk and swear blue fire! *(He imitates a parrot's squawk.) Stand by and go about! Hang him from the yard-arm! Pieces of eight! Pieces of eight!* That's her favourite, and no wonder, the ill-gained gold she must've seen in her time. *Pieces of eight!*

(JIM and SILVER laugh.)

120

Two hundred years old, Jim. And she'll be squawking still, I reckon, when we're all of us long gone and meat for the worms or the fishes.

(He rises, takes up his crutch and goes, leaving JIM sitting alone. HANDS speaks to JIM.)

HANDS	Aye. An uncommon man, is Long John. You stay alongside of him, young Hawkins, and you'll come to no harm.

(HANDS turns from JIM and goes. He's followed by REDCAP, TOM MORGAN, and DICK.)

Captain England *A famous, real-life pirate.*

yard-arm *The yard was the crosspiece slung across the mast from which the sails were hung. The yard-arm were the ends of the yard. Sailors executed at sea (a not uncommon event) were hanged from the yard-arm.*

pieces of eight *Name for a golden Spanish dollar.*

ACT 2 ❖ SCENE 7

ADULT JIM narrates.

ADULT JIM   For harm there was, waiting to be done, skulking like a rat
in the black bilges of men's hearts. And it was by chance I
discovered it, on the last day of our voyage, when I went
down into the hold to get an apple from the barrel.

*(JIM goes down to the lower part of the stage. He gets an apple,
and sits among the jumble of timber, eating.)*

It was just after sundown. My duties were done. On deck,
the watch was forward, looking out for the island. We knew
we'd sight it soon, and all spirits were high. We had a
steady breeze and a quiet sea, the only sound was the swish   1●
of the waves against our bows, and there in the dark,
comfortable and warm, rocked by the gentle motion of the
ship, I fell aleep. Only to be woken, moments later, by the
sound of voices. The sound of *his* voice.

*(JIM has been falling asleep during the above. Now, SILVER and
DICK enter, SILVER speaking.)*

SILVER   No. Not I. Flint was captain. I was quartermaster, along of
my timber leg. Same broadside I lost my leg, old Pew lost
his deadlights. *The Walrus*, that was Flint's ship, and I've
seen her decks running red with blood and fit to sink with   2●
gold.

DICK   He was the flower of the flock, Flint was, so I've heard tell.

SILVER   You've heard well right enough, Dick. Flint's men was the

---

quartermaster *The man on board ship responsible for giving out the crew's
rations.*

broadside *When a ship fires all the guns along one side of its deck at once.*

lost his deadlights *Lost his eyes.*

---

roughest crew afloat, and feared of Flint, they was, every
man of them. But Flint his own self was feared of me. And
where's Flint now? Died of rum at Savannah. Where's Pew?
Died a beggar-man. Where's Billy Bones? Died like a dog
with his heart burst. And the rest of Flint's men, where are
they? Aboard this ship, what's left of them, and not one
them with ha'penny-piece to buy a shot of grog.   30

DICK   The way you put it, there ain't much use to the life, if that's
what it comes to.

SILVER   It ain't much use for fools, sure enough. But I ain't no fool,
and neither are you, Dick. Smart, you are. Smart as paint.
I knowed that the minute I clapped eyes on you. And that's
why I'm talking to you, now, like a man. Here. Take a shot
of this grog.

DICK   Thanks. I will.

(SILVER hands DICK a flask. DICK takes a swig from it.)

SILVER   Here's how it is with gentlemen of fortune, Dick. They lives   40
rough and risks swinging, but when a cruise is done, it's
hundreds of pounds instead of farthings they have in their
pockets. Now, the most of them goes for rum and a good
fling, and then it's off to sea again in their shirts. But that's
not the course I lay. It ain't the making of the money, you
see, it's the saving of it that counts. Two thousand I made,
sailing with Flint. That ain't bad for a man before the mast,
is it?

DICK   It ain't bad at all, Long John.

SILVER   And do you know where that two thousand might be now?   50
Why my missis has it, and the *Spyglass* is sold, and the old
girl's off to meet me, and I ain't telling a living soul, not

---

farthing *The smallest, and least valuable of English coins.*

two thousand *Two thousand pounds, he means. Worth a lot more in his
day than ours. Silver was a very rich man!*

even you, Dick, where that place might be. For this is to be my last voyage, and when I'm home from it, I'll set myself up as a gentleman, in earnest. Do you see now what kind of man it is you'll be signing up to sail along?

DICK Aye, I do. I'll tell you, Long John, I didn't half a quarter like this job till I had this talk with you. But now – here's my hand on it.

(DICK holds out his hand. SILVER clasps it.) 6

SILVER A brave lad you are, and a smart one too. Smart as paint! Let's have another swig of that grog to seal our bargain.

(He takes the flask from DICK, drinks, then hands it back to DICK, who drinks. At the same time, ISRAEL HANDS and REDCAP enter. SILVER turns to them.)

SILVER Dick's square, lads.

HANDS We knowed Dick was square. Didn't we, Redcap?

REDCAP Yes. He's no fool, is Dick. But what we wants to know, Barbecue, is how long are we going to stand off?

HANDS That's right. I've had enough of that captain, for one. I want to get into that cabin. I wants me hands on his brandy and his wine. 7

SILVER Your two heads ain't much account, and never was. But I reckon you're able to hear, well enough, and maybe understand what I say. And what I say is, we'll stand off till I give the word!

REDCAP And when'll that be?

SILVER The last moment I can manage, that's when. It's not us that has the map. It's that there Squire or the Doctor, and I

  Dick's square *Dick's with us.*

	mean to have them to find the treasure for us, and ship it aboard. So what I say is this. We'll go along with them sweet and gentle till the treasure's stowed. And then – let her rip!	80
REDCAP	That's the tune I like. Let her rip!	
HANDS	Dead men don't bite.	
DICK	All of them?	
SILVER	All that ain't with us.	
HANDS	And the boy? Him as you seem to be so fond of? He's the one that done us out of the map, and got old Pew killed into the bargain. Besides, I hates boys. Let me deal with him . . .	90
SILVER	You leave the boy to me, Israel! I'll see that he tells no tales. Now. Let's drink to our enterprise.	

(SILVER hands round the flask. Each drinks in turn.)

REDCAP	To luck.	
HANDS	To old Flint.	
DICK	To gold.	
SILVER	And here's to Long John, and his last voyage.	

(As they drink, ADULT JIM narrates.)

ADULT JIM	So they drank to our deaths, and I sat there, listening to them, listening to his voice, plotting bloodshed and murder. It made me sick to my soul – and the next minute, there and then, I was in fear for my life.	100
SILVER	Dick. Jump up, like a sweet lad, and fetch me an apple from the barrel over there.	
DICK	Aye, aye, Long John.	

(DICK rises and moves towards where JIM is hiding.)

ADULT JIM	My heart leapt in my chest as I heard him rise, his footsteps

coming towards me. There was no escape, I knew I was done for – then came a cry from above that turned fate in my favour. 110

(Above, one of the SAILORS calls out.)

1st SAILOR   Land! Land ho!

DICK stops, turns.

HANDS   We're there!

REDCAP   The island!

SILVER   That's it, lads! Up on deck and lets get a sight of her.

(SILVER, HANDS, REDCAP and DICK go to the upper level, as the 1st SAILOR calls out again.)

1st SAILOR   Land ho! 120

(All gather on the deck of the ship, now – SAILORS, PIRATES, TRELAWNEY, LIVESEY, HUNTER and SMOLLETT and, last of all, JIM. SMOLLETT calls up to the 1st SAILOR.)

SMOLLETT   Where away?

1st SAILOR   There! Off to the port bow!

(All peer outwards towards the approaching island, as ADULT JIM narrates.)

ADULT JIM   I came up from the hold to find them all gathered on deck. The sun had set now, and the moon was up, and out to the south-west, we saw two hills rising, black against the sky. 130

SMOLLETT   Has anyone ever seen that land ahead?

SILVER   I have, sir. I've watered there with a trader. Those two hills there, the one's called Foremast Hill, the other they call the Spyglass. There's a bay between them we used for anchorage.

SMOLLETT   Thank you, Silver. We may need your help later on, once we've gone ashore.

SILVER	And happy I'll be to give it, sir.
ADULT JIM	Then his eye fell on me, and he came across, smiling, and clapped his hand on my shoulder and gripped it tight, and 140 it was all I could do to keep from shuddering.

(SILVER speaks to JIM.)

SILVER	Do you see it, Jim? This here's a sweet spot, this island – a sweet spot for a lad to get ashore on. You'll swim, and you'll climb trees, and you'll hunt goats, you will; and you'll go aloft them hills like a goat yourself. Why, it makes me young again. I could almost forget my timber leg. Ah, Jim, it's a pleasant thing to be young and full of the joys of life.

(All remain gazing outwards, as chorus of SAILORS narrates.)   150

1st SAILOR	And we gaze out into the glimmering dark . . .
2nd SAILOR	Where there's no sound, only the whisper of wind . . .
3rd SAILOR	And the hush of the waves on the far shore . . .
4th SAILOR	As the island rises like a ghost from the sea . . .
5th SAILOR	Moon-washed, mist-lit, a place of enchantment . . .
6th SAILOR	And fevered dreams, and sudden death.

(Lights fade slowly to blackout.)

CHARACTER AND LANGUAGE Look closely at Israel Hands' lines in Scene 6. What can you tell about his character from the way he speaks, and what he says? What does he say that tells us he has known Silver for a long time? Make notes on the character of Israel Hands, and write down examples from what he says that support your ideas.

DISCUSSION AND CHARACTER Silver's story of the parrot serves no dramatic function in Scene 6 – in other words, it does not move the action forward, or add to the plot.

As a class, discuss why you think the story is there, and what purpose you think it serves. What does it tell us about Silver's character, and his relationship with Jim?

ARTWORK Storyboard the voyage of the *Hispaniola* as if for a film. Sketch four frames showing different moments from the voyage (these moments may not be in the play – a storm, for example). Also, make notes on what the audience would hear in frame, what the camera would be doing, and how you would show visually the passage of time.

ACTING Create a short scene between Doctor Livesey and Squire Trelawney. This takes place just after Livesey has had his drink of rum in Scene 6, and the Squire is still infuriated with Captain Smollett. This could be in twos or, if you decide to add Hunter to the scene, in threes.

DISCUSSION AND WRITING In groups, discuss what more you have learned about Flint and his crew from Silver's conversation with Dick. See if you can start to piece together, and write, the story of Flint and his crew, the buried treasure, Flint's death, and the map.

DISCUSSION Silver says to Dick: 'But Flint his own self was afeared of me.'
    As a class, discuss if you think this statement is true, or if Silver is just trying to impress Dick. If you think it is true, what is it about Silver that would make Flint scared of him?

HOT-SEATING In small groups, one takes on the role of Dick, and the others question him as to why he wanted to join the pirates, and what it was that finally persuaded him to do it.

WRITING Imagine you're Jim, sitting in the dark of the hold and listening to Silver and the others hatch their plot. Write down your immediate thoughts and feelings as a monologue, in prose or poetry.

ACTING In this scene, Jim discovers the truth about Silver, and that, all the time, he had been deceiving him and the others. In small groups, create a short scene in which one person discovers an unpleasant truth about someone they liked or admired.

WRITING Hunter is keeping a journal, or diary, of the voyage for a friend or relation at home. Write some or all of this journal, making a note of all the main events of the voyage from setting sail to sighting the island, as seen through Hunter's eyes. Also make a note of his thoughts, feelings, and hopes.

ARTWORK Sketch a single frame from a film storyboard of the sighting of the island. Use the text to give you information for this. Decide what the camera will be seeing – just the island, for example, or the crew gazing at the island, or a long shot of the ship approaching the island. Make notes on what would be heard on the soundtrack. Think carefully about the visual effect you want to create.

THE ISLAND
ACT 3 ❖ SCENE 1

ADULT JIM and BOY JIM enter. They stand on raised areas, on opposite sides of the stage. SILVER is below, centre stage, but still, and unlit.

ADULT JIM	In my dream, I'm running through a thick forest, hot, sweating, my heart thumping. I stumble, trip, drag myself to my feet again, plunge on through the undergrowth. But where am I going? Why am I so afraid? What is it I'm running from?	1
JIM	Them. I'm running from them. I have to get away from them!	
ADULT JIM	Struggling uphill, leaves lashing my face, close heat, biting insects, and the shrieks of birds like gunshots around me . . .	10
JIM	But they are gunshots! And those cries are the cries of men dying!	
ADULT JIM	And I'm out in the light again, the glaring light, blinding me at first, and I hear voices somewhere below, and I rub my eyes, and I look, from the top of the slope, through the clearing in the trees, down to a tangled, swampy hollow . . .	
JIM	They're killing the men! The ones who wouldn't join them! Down there in the marshes, they're killing them!	
ADULT JIM	And he's there, I can see him, kneeling, bending over something, his crutch on the ground, and he's doing something to whatever he's kneeling on . . . then all at once he looks up, into the light, and he's grinning, and his hands are covered in blood . . .	20
JIM	And there's a knife in the back of the body on the ground!	

(The light comes up suddenly on SILVER.)

SILVER It had to be done. A man can't flinch from doing what's necessary, when the time comes. Dooty is dooty, Jim, and dead men don't bite. But you understand that. A smart lad, like you, smart as paint. You understand Long John more than you let on, don't you? You know what's in his heart, **30** what makes his blood sing. Not the treasure, not that alone. It's the very thrill of it, Jim. Excitement! Adventure! The thrill of the chase and the kill!

(BOY JIM cries out.)

JIM No! This no dream! This is real! I'm on the island, and it's really happening!

(SILVER goes. ADULT JIM turns to the audience.)

ADULT JIM No dream. It was real. I was on the island. It was really happening. And this is how it came about.

DISCUSSION This scene is written in a 'non-naturalistic' way. You are back in Jim's dream-world, and events are narrated, in a dream-like way, by both Adult Jim and Boy Jim. As a class, discuss why you think the playwright chose to open Act 3 in this way.

DISCUSSION In small groups, discuss what you think Silver is saying about Jim's character in his speech to him at the end of the scene? What more does the speech tell us about Silver's character?

CHARACTER Add any new characters to your list, and make notes on them. Also add extra notes to characters already in the file.

ACT 3 ❖ SCENE 2

As ADULT JIM narrates, TRELAWNEY, LIVESEY, HUNTER and SMOLLETT enter to JIM, for a flashback scene, on board the ship, in the CAPTAIN's cabin, the night before the events above. BOY JIM moves down from the raised area to join them.

ADULT JIM	The island had been sighted. By the light of the full moon, our ship drew closer towards it. All was quiet on deck. The Captain, the Doctor, and the Squire went below. I followed them. And, in the safety of the cabin, I told them all that I'd heard in the hold, of Silver's betrayal, and the great danger our lives were in. For a time after, all were silent, and then the Squire spoke up.
TRELAWNEY	Captain Smollett. You were right, and I was wrong. I've been a fool. You have my apologies, and I await your orders.
SMOLLETT	I've been a fool myself not to see any sign of this mutiny. How they've kept it so quiet beats me.
LIVESEY	That's Silver's doing. For all his villainy, he's a remarkable man.
SMOLLETT	He'd look remarkably well hanging from a yard-arm! But this is all talk, and leads to nothing. Thanks to the boy, here, we know the situation we're in. The point is, what are we to do about it?
TRELAWNEY	We'll stand or fall by your advice, Captain Smollett.
SMOLLETT	First of all, we must go on to the island. If I gave the word to turn about, they would rise at once.
LIVESEY	Very true.

Line numbers: 1, 10, 20

 turn about *Turn the ship round – go back.*

SMOLLETT	Second, we have time before us, at least until the treasure is found. And, according to what Jim has said, there are faithful hands on board.
TRELAWNEY	How many, though? We don't know that.
HUNTER	You have me, sir . . .
TRELAWNEY	Yes, we know that, Hunter . . .
HUNTER	And there are three more I can name I'd swear are honest men. 30
SMOLLETT	That's something. But it leaves the odds very much in Silver's favour. So, what I propose is this. We'll reach the anchorage tomorrow morning. I'll tell Silver he can take the men ashore. After so long aboard they'll be eager to go. We'll remain with the ship, so we'll have that at least, and the weapons.
LIVESEY	Won't Silver suspect something?
SMOLLETT	There's no reason why he should. And Jim's told us he means to keep his hand until the treasure's been found. He'll bring them all back on board mild as lambs, you mark 40 my words. And that's when we'll take them, when they least suspect it. If it's a fight they want, by God, they'll get it, but at a time of our choosing, and to our advantage!
	(TRELAWNEY, SMOLLETT, LIVESEY and HUNTER go. JIM remains onstage. ADULT JIM narrates.)
ADULT JIM	It seemed a good plan on the face of it. But, like all plans, it could take no account of the unexpected. For, when the sun rose the next morning, when we'd anchored off the island, and the longboat was lowered, I took it into my head to join the shore party. 50
	(BOY JIM speaks his thoughts.)
JIM	They won't need me on board. A boy's no use to them. And there are trees to climb, and hills to scale, and cool springs and pools . . . a whole world of adventure!

ADULT JIM	A whole world of adventure. It called to me and I answered it. At the last minute I climbed into the longboat, sat next to Silver the whole journey, and, as soon as the longboat touched the shore, leapt from the prow, and I was off , racing up the beach . . .
JIM	Plunging into the trees . . .
ADULT JIM	Silver's cries growing faint behind me . . .
JIM	Hot, sweating, my heart thumping . . .
ADULT JIM	Struggling uphill, leaves lashing my face, roots snagging my heels, close heat, biting insects, and the shrieks of birds like gunshots around me . . .
JIM	But they are gunshots! And those cries are the cries of men dying! They're killing the men! The ones who wouldn't join them! Down there in the marshes, they're killing them!
ADULT JIM	Too late I saw the folly of my action. For my friends were on the ship, and the enemy was abroad, and I was alone on that murderous island!

60

70

CHARACTER When Captain Smollett, Doctor Livesey and Squire Trelawney discover how Silver has deceived them, each reacts in a slightly different way.

As a class, discuss these different reactions to Silver. What do their reactions tells us about the characters of these three men?

WRITING Imagine you're Jim, looking back on the events in Act 3, Scene 1. Write an explanation of why you suddenly took it into your heard to go to the island.

ARTWORK Storyboard four of the main events from Act 3, Scenes 1 and 2 as if for a film. Sketch each frame, and make notes on what the audience will be hearing, and what the camera will be doing.

ACT 3 ❖ SCENE 3

The CHORUS enters, keeping back and in shadow. They are now the voices of the island.

1st VOICE	But is he? Is he really alone?
2nd VOICE	Or is there someone else there?
3rd VOICE	Someone, or something else there?
4th VOICE	A shadow in the shadows . . .
5th VOICE	A whisper in the leaves . . .
6th VOICE	A figure, flickering amongst the trees.
	(JIM calls out, looking around him.)
JIM	Who's there?
	(The CHORUS speaks together.)
ALL	Who's there?
JIM	Who is it?
ALL	Who is it?
JIM	Who are you?
ALL	Who are you?
JIM	Where are you?
	(CHORUS speaks individually.)
1st VOICE	Here.
2nd VOICE	Here.
3rd VOICE	Here.
4th VOICE	Here.
5th VOICE	Here.

6th VOICE	Here.
	(BEN GUNN suddenly appears.)
BEN GUNN	Here, boy!
	(JIM turns, with a cry.)
	Have you come with that ship? That ship, anchored off there. I seen her come in. Have you come with her?
JIM	Yes . . .
BEN GUNN	Is she Flint's ship? Tell me true, boy!
JIM	No . . . but there are some of Flint's men aboard . . .
BEN GUNN	I knew it! I could smell 'em! And is among them . . . a man with one leg?
JIM	You mean Silver?
BEN GUNN	Yes! Silver! I mean him! Silver! Was you sent by him, boy? If you was, I'm as good as pork!
JIM	No. I want nothing to do with him, or the rest of Flint's men. There are honest men too aboard that ship . . .
BEN GUNN	And be you one of them honest men?
JIM	I hope so . . .
BEN GUNN	But you ain't sure, is that it? Well, I'll tell you, boy. You have an honest look about you. So, you tell me, what be honest-men doing putting in at this island?

30

40

50

73

JIM	We have a map of Flint's treasure . . .
BEN GUNN	His map? You have Flint's map?
JIM	Yes . . .
BEN GUNN	And you've come a-looking for his treasure. Come a-looking to dig it up again . . .
JIM	That's right . . .
BEN GUNN	And he'd take it from you. Silver. He'd take it from you and cut your throats. Is that the right of it?
JIM	More or less . . .
BEN GUNN	I know it is! I know Mr John Silver and his crooked ways. For they was mine, once, they was. I walked his path. But not no more, no. For look what it's brought me to! See where wickedness has brought poor Ben Gunn!
JIM	Is that your name?
BEN GUNN	Ben Gunn, aye, and I haven't spoken to a human soul for three years. None that was living, anyways. And how do I come to be here, eh? Shipwrecked, says you? No, says I. Not shipwrecked. Marooned! Marooned three years gone! Tell me, boy! Answer me true! You wouldn't have any cheese about you, would you?
JIM	Cheese? No . . .
BEN GUNN	I guessed you wouldn't. A piece of cheese, is all I wants. Goats and berries and oysters I have, but no cheese. There's many a long night I've dreamed of cheese – toasted cheese – and then I've woke, and I'm here – and then I've wept to dream again . . .

6((marginal line number)

7((marginal line number)

Marooned *Left alone, either by accident or, as in Ben Gunn's case, on purpose, on an island.*

(He sits, forlorn, and appears for the moment to have forgotten JIM. ADULT JIM narrates.)

ADULT JIM   And he sat on the ground, a ragged, scorched, scarecrow of
a man – and I felt such pity for him, so forlorn and desolate   80
he seemed . . . like a creature from some old tale, the
outcast and outlawed king of the island . . .

(GUNN looks up suddenly.)

BEN GUNN   I sailed with Flint in the days I was a sinner. I were in Flint's
ship when he came ashore and buried the treasure. Six men
he took with him, and the treasure, and they was gone a
week, and us standing off in the old *Walrus*, just where your
ship is now. Then one evening as the sun was setting, we
seen the boat coming back, and only him in it. Flint, alone!
And where was the other six, says you? Dead, says I. Dead   90
and buried along of the treasure.

JIM   Dead men don't bite.

BEN GUNN   Aye! That's true! Killed them all, he did. How, I don't know.
But he done it. And it makes me go cold still to think of it.
That was my last voyage with Flint. I wanted no more of
him. The Devil he was, and I didn't want to sail with him
to hell. So I slipped ship and joined a merchantman, and I
never seen Flint nor his crew again.

JIM   Then how was it you were left here?

BEN GUNN   I'd done with Flint, but he hadn't done with me. That other   100
ship I was in, three years back we sighted this island. 'Boys,'
says I, 'here's Flint's treasure! Let's land and find it!' Twelve
days we looked for it, and two men died of the fever, and
one fine morning the others turns to me, and they says,
'Here, Ben Gunn,' they says, 'here's a musket, and shot, and

merchantman *A merchant ship, which was a trading ship as opposed to a naval ship.*

a spade and a pickaxe. You can find Flint's money for yourself,' they says. And they sailed off and left me here, and here's where I've been ever since.

JIM   I promise you, Ben Gunn, if things turn out well for us, and if we ever get away from this island, we'll take you with us.   11C

BEN GUNN   Them's honest words, lad, honest words from a gentleman. But are they just your words, eh? What about them others aboard? Are they as honest as you?

JIM   They're all gentlemen. They'll say the same as me.

BEN GUNN   They will, will they? Well, now, when you see them again, you'll tell them gentlemen – 'Here's Ben Gunn,' says you, 'as sailed with Flint – Ben Gunn three years on this island – and he knows the island, he does,' says you, 'and all her secrets, he knows – all of them, mark you – for he's been here three years and uncovered them all'. Do you take my   12(
meaning?

JIM   I'm . . . not sure . . .

BEN GUNN   All of them! Dug right down to her blessed bones, I have! And I wants none of them! They're a curse and a damnation to a man like me. You tell your gentlemen, all Ben Gunn wants is his passage home, which he'll pay for like an honest man. That's all, lad. To be off this cursed island. And a piece of cheese. An honest piece of cheese. You makes sure you tell your gentlemen that!

JIM   I will . . . if I can ever get back to them . . .   13(

BEN GUNN   'If!' says you. 'And why that 'if'?', says I. ' 'Cos I have no boat,' says you. 'But I have,' says I.

JIM   A boat . . . ?

BEN GUNN   I made it myself! Sticks and goat-skins! You see the white rock? That's where you'll find her. Under the white rock! But you promise me this, boy. If you was to see Silver again, you wouldn't tell him about Ben Gunn, would you? Wild

	horses wouldn't drag it from you, would they?	
JIM	No.	
BEN GUNN	Your word on it!	**140**
JIM	I give you my word.	
BEN GUNN	You're a good lad. And mind this. If any of old Flint's crew camp ashore . . . don't be surprised if there's widows in the morning!	

(He suddenly turns from JIM and starts to clamber up one of the raised areas.)

JIM	Wait . . . !	
BEN GUNN	Don't you forget, now! Tell your gentlemen. If Ben Gunn's wanted, they'll know where to find him. Which is where he found you. Tell them to come looking, and they'll find him. Ben Gunn! Poor Ben Gunn, king of the island!	**150**

(He goes.)

ADULT JIM	And he was gone, clambering up over the rocks like a goat himself, his figure fading into the shadow, melting back into leaf and tree. And once more, I was alone.	

(CHORUS speaks, as voices of the island. They exit on their lines.)

1st VOICE	Then the air splits wide . . .	
2nd VOICE	The trees seem to shake . . .	
3rd VOICE	Birds fly, shrieking into the air . . .	
4th VOICE	As the whole island's rocked by the sound of thunder . . .	**160**
5th VOICE	Cracking its doom across the clear blue sky . . .	
6th VOICE	The thunder of a cannon-shot from across the bay.	
ADULT JIM	And once more I'm off and running . . .	
JIM	Scrambling through undergrowth, pushing through the trees . . .	

ADULT JIM   Like someone stumbling from one bad dream to
                another . . .

JIM   And I don't know how long I'm running for, like all day, it
                seems . . .

ADULT JIM   As the sky grows red as if streaked with blood . . .   17(

JIM   And I see a clearing down below me, and there's a wooden
                stockade there, and a Union Jack fluttering at the top of a
                flagpole . . . !

ADULT JIM   And the sound of gunshot crackles above the trees!

DISCUSSION AND ARTWORK/WRITING Up till now, the Chorus
have taken on a variety of 'real' roles – locals and sailors. But what role
do they take in this scene?

As a class, discuss how you would best describe this role, what the
purpose of it is, why the playwright has written them like he has. Then, using
these ideas, imagine you're staging this scene for the theatre.

How would you costume the 'voices', and where would you position them
onstage? Either make a sketch or written notes to show your ideas.

LANGUAGE Ben Gunn has a very particular way of speaking. His thoughts seem
to jump from one thing to the other, and he often speaks of himself in the third
person.

In small groups, discuss why you think he speaks in this way. What does the
way he speaks tell you about his character?

ACTING In small groups, create the scene where the sailors decide to maroon
Ben Gunn on the island. End the scene with the ship sailing off, leaving Ben Gunn
alone.

DISCUSSION In small groups, discuss what you think Ben Gunn means when he
says: ' . . . don't be surprised if there's widows in the morning.'

ACT 3 ❖ SCENE 4

LIVESEY enters, and narrates. ADULT JIM and JIM stand to one side, watching.

LIVESEY Not long after the longboat had gone ashore – and when   1
we learned that Jim Hawkins had gone ashore also, we
heard the cries of men and gunshots coming from the
island.

(TRELAWNEY enters and narrates.)

TRELAWNEY The killing had begun, sooner than we had anticipated, and
we knew action must be taken. For to remain on board the
ship would put us all in grave danger.

(HUNTER enters and narrates. He is armed with a musket.)

HUNTER So we armed ourselves from the weapons store and Captain   10
Smollett and myself went on deck, and he spoke to those
pirates who'd been left behind.

(SMOLLETT enters, and calls out. He is armed with two pistols.)

SMOLLETT Mr Hands!

(HANDS enters, and speaks insolently to SMOLLETT.)

HANDS Aye, aye . . . Captain.

SMOLLETT Mr Hands. Here are two of us armed with pistol and
musket. We intend to go ashore, and to take the rest of the
weapons and provisions with us. If any man of yours
attempts to prevent us, that man is dead. Keep your musket   20
trained on them, Hunter, until we're done, then come
aboard yourself. And don't hesitate to fire if needs be.

HUNTER I won't, Captain Smollett

(He keeps his musket trained on HANDS. HANDS narrates.)

HANDS So we let them go. What else could we do? There weren't
enough of us left aboard to make a fight of it. Especially

against Long John's orders. And, what's more, they had all the weapons. Excepting one. We had the ship's gun.

(TOM MORGAN enters and narrates.)

MORGAN   And Israel here had been Flint's gunner. And a proper master gunner he was.   30

(REDCAP enters and narrates.)

REDCAP   And as soon as they was loaded and away in the longboat, we primed that gun and rammed down the shot . . .

(At this point HUNTER lowers his musket.)

MORGAN   And Israel took a bearing . . .

HANDS   A little higher lads . . .

REDCAP   And touched the fuse . . .

HANDS   And we blasted them clean out the water!

(HANDS, MORGAN and REDCAP give a cheer, then go.   40
LIVESEY continues to narrate.)

LIVESEY   Luckily for us, the shot fell a little wide, and, though the boat was destroyed, and half our provisions lost, we managed at least to escape with our lives.

TRELAWNEY Then we made our way up from the beach towards the stockade in the forest we'd seen marked on the map.

HUNTER   But before we reached there, we heard a cry go up, and shots were fired, and we saw the mutineers approaching from out of the trees.

SMOLLETT So we made a running fight of it, shooting as we ran . . .   50

LIVESEY   Sending out a volley that brought down two of their number . . .

TRELAWNEY And sent the rest of the pack scuttling back into the woods . . .

HUNTER	Then we came to the clearing and climbed the stockade fence . . .
SMOLLETT	And secured ourselves in the log-house against the next attack.
ADULT JIM	Which was where I found them, a little while later. And never was I so glad to see them, nor they me, for they feared I'd been killed. And I told them my story, and they told me theirs.

60

(JIM approaches the stockade company, and is greeted warmly. At the same time, CHORUS 1 and 2 enter as two SAILORS, GREY and JOYCE. They carry weapons. Throughout the following, all onstage prepare for the attack, building a makeshift barricade from items onstage.)

LIVESEY	It's lucky you came when you did, Jim. Those villains will launch a full attack on us before long. And we shall want all the help we can get.

70

HUNTER	Can you fire a pistol or a musket, Jim?
JIM	I don't know, Mister Hunter – I've never had call to before . . .
TRELAWNEY	Now's the time for him to learn, then. Eh, Captain Smollett?
SMOLLETT	I'd rather he didn't. What we need is men we can rely on to hit their target – marksmen like yourself and Hunter and these others here. I'm no shot myself. Jim and I will be better employed keeping the weapons loaded. Though, if it comes to a bit of rough and tumble, we'll be ready and able to swing a cutlass.

80

(He hands a cutlass to JIM. JIM takes it, a little nervously.)

TRELAWNEY	As ever, I bow to your greater experience in these matters, Captain.
JIM	What are the odds, do you think? Do we stand a chance?

SMOLLETT	I'll be honest. When it comes to numbers the odds are at present well in their favour . . .
LIVESEY	They're two less than they were.
SMOLLETT	True, Doctor. And we have the log-house, and the fence – they'll have to climb that to get to us. And we have Grey and Joyce here who've elected to side with us – and they're no strangers to warfare.
GREY	We'll give them a fight if they come looking for it.
JOYCE	And with pleasure, after the way they tried to force us into joining with them.
TRELAWNEY	We're well-placed for a siege here. And they must come at us in the open, clear targets every one of them.
LIVESEY	And there's fever on this island. The swamps are full of it. It's my belief that, if we can hold them off for a while, they'll lose heart, and give the whole thing up as a lost cause. Ruffians like those have no real stomach for adversity.
SMOLLETT	That might be true of most of them, Doctor. But not Silver. He's staked his life on this enterprise of his. Fever and resistance won't shake him so easily. Never underestimate Silver. The man is a formidable enemy.
	(JOYCE, who has been keeping watch, turns to SMOLLETT.)
JOYCE	Talk of the devil and he comes, sir. He's here.
SMOLLETT	What?
JOYCE	Silver. Making his way towards us.
SMOLLETT	Alone?
JOYCE	There's one with him – carrying a white flag.
TRELAWNEY	What's the villain up to now?
SMOLLETT	Ten to one it's a trick of some kind. Take up your weapons and keep inside

90

100

110

(GREY, JOYCE, TRELAWNEY and HUNTER take up pistols and muskets. SILVER enters, on the other side of the barricade, accompanied by DICK, who's carrying a piece of white sheeting tied to a branch. He calls out.)

SILVER	Ahoy there! Captain Smollett . . . !	120

(SMOLLETT aims a pistol at SILVER.)

SMOLLETT That's far enough, Silver!

SILVER Flag of truce, Captain! I'm unarmed!

SMOLLETT What do you want with your flag of truce?

SILVER Captain Silver asking permission to come aboard and talk terms.

SMOLLETT Captain Silver, is it? I don't know him. Who's Captain Silver?

SILVER These poor lads have chosen me as their captain, sir – after your desertion . . .   130

TRELAWNEY Desertion! The audacity of the man . . . !

SILVER But we're willing to submit, if we can come to terms. All I ask is your word, Captain Smollett, to give me safe passage in and out of this stockade, and a minute to get out of shot before a gun is fired.

SMOLLETT I have no wish to talk to you, Silver. But, if you wish to talk to me, your way's clear. There'll be no treachery on our side. And you'll come alone.

SILVER A word from you is enough, Captain. I know a gentleman when I see one, you may lay to that. *(To DICK.)* Plant that   140 flag of truce in the ground there, Dick, and go back to the others. I'll be safe enough here.

(DICK places the flag of truce upright and goes. SILVER makes his way to the barricade. He sees JIM.)

Jim! Here you be! That was a pretty trick you played this

morning, skipping off out the boat as you did. What have you been up to all the day? Climbing trees and chasing goats, I'll be bound.

JIM   No, Silver. I've been watching murder committed.

SILVER   Have you, now? Here. Take my crutch while I climb across.   150

(JIM takes SILVER's crutch and SILVER climbs over the barricade and takes his crutch again. He looks around.)

There. And here's the Doctor and the Squire, all of you together like one happy family. And Mr Grey and Mr Joyce. I'll lay it was you dropped two of my lads just now . . .

SMOLLETT   Enough of that. Sit down, and say what you have to say.

SILVER   I will, so long as somebody gives me a hand up again. *(He sits.)* Right you are, Captain Smollett. Dooty is dooty, and here it is. We want that treasure, and we mean to have it. And you'd just as soon keep all your lives, I reckon. So it   160 comes to this. Give us Flint's chart, and we'll offer you a choice. Either you can come aboard of us, once the treasure's shipped, and I'll give you my affydavy to set you somewhere safe ashore. Or, if that ain't to your fancy, we'll divide stores with you, man for man, and I'll give you my affydavy to speak the first ship I sight and send them here to pick you up. That's my offer, and handsomer you couldn't look to get.

SMOLLETT   Is that all?

SILVER   Every last word, by thunder! Refuse that, and you've seen   170 the last of me but musket-balls.

SMOLLETT   Very good. Now hear me. If you'll come up, one by one, and unarmed, I'll engage to clap you all in irons and take

my affydavy *He means affidavit, which is a written statement confirmed by an oath, and legally binding.*

you home to a fair trial in England. If you won't, I'll see you all to Davy Jones. You can't find the treasure and you can't sail the ship. You're on a lee shore, Master Silver, and these are the last words you'll get from me. For, in the name of heaven, the next time I meet you I'll put a bullet through your back!

(SILVER stares for a moment at SMOLLETT, then raises his arm.) 180

SILVER   Give me a hand up.

SMOLLETT   Not I.

SILVER   Who'll give me a hand up!

(He looks at them all. No one moves.)

Jim?

(He offers his hand to JIM. JIM hesitates, but does not take it.)

Damn you, then! Damn all your souls to hell!

(He struggles up, using his crutch, and clambers back over the barricade, then turns, and spits.) 190

There! That's what I think of you! Laugh, by thunder! Before an hour's out, you'll laugh on the other side! Them that die'll be the lucky ones!

(He goes, tearing down the white flag, and throwing it on to the floor.)

---

see you all to Davy Jones *Davy Jones's Locker was, in seamen's slang, the bottom of the sea – to be sent to Davy Jones's Locker meant to be drowned.*

on a lee shore *A shore on to which the wind is blowing from such a direction as to make it very difficult for a sailing vessel to sail straight out to sea, into the wind.*

LANGUAGE AND ACTING For the first part of this scene, Jim's arrival at the stockade, all events are shown through a mixture of narrative and stage action. In other words, some events are narrated by characters in the scene, and some are acted. There are therefore two kinds of language in the scene: narrative and dialogue.

In small groups, try acting out this scene, and see if you can find a way of showing the difference between when the characters are narrating, and when they're involved in the action. This could also be shown with the way they move, and where they stand in the scene.

ARTWORK Storyboard the events in Scene 4, up to the moment when Doctor Livesey and the others reach the island. Choose what you think are the four most exciting moments, and create frames for them, with notes on what sounds would be heard, what dialogue is being spoken, and what the camera is doing.

DISCUSSION Silver tries to make a bargain with the stockade party.

In small groups, discuss whether you think he intends to keep his part of the bargain. Give good reasons for your opinion, drawn from what you know of Silver's character.

FREEZE-FRAME In groups, freeze-frame the moment when the stockade party see Silver approaching. Each person speaks their thoughts and feelings at that particular moment.

You could also make a drawing of this freeze-frame, with thought-bubbles for each character.

DISCUSSION As a class, discuss what you think the effect on the audience would be when no one will help Silver to stand? Will it make us pity him? If so, how might this change the audience's view of Silver?

What do you think the playwright's intention is?

ACT 3 ❖ SCENE 5

A drumbeat sounds, steady, slow. CHORUS 3 – 6 join the PIRATES. The PIRATES and the stockade party assemble in two groups, on separate parts of the stage, and face out to the audience. As the drumbeat continues they narrate the attack and the fight.

GREY	We take up our weapons . . .	1
JOYCE	Prepare for the fight . . .	
SMOLLETT	And wait, eyes fixed on the ground ahead.	
LIVESEY	Then there's a cry . . .	
HUNTER	And a gunshot . . .	
TRELAWNEY	And the air explodes.	
JIM	And death comes howling out of the trees!	
CHORUS 3	And the muskets crack!	
CHORUS 4	And the swordblades flash!	
CHORUS 5	And the air hangs thick with powder and smoke!	10
CHORUS 6	And out of the smoke we come racing towards them!	
REDCAP	Death in our eyes . . .	
DICK	Death in our hearts . . .	
MORGAN	Hungry for blood . . .	
MERRY	Hungry for slaughter . . .	
HANDS	And the cry goes up and the fight's on!	
	(The drumbeat gets faster.)	
GREY	Blindly we fire!	
CHORUS 3	Men scream and fall!	
CHORUS 4	A bullet in the face!	20

JOYCE	A backbone smashed!
CHORUS 5	Musket-balls crash through sunlight and flesh!
CHORUS 6	The air hangs thick with powder and smoke!
SMOLLETT	And we take up our swords . . .
DICK	And it's hand to hand . . .
LIVESEY	We hack and we cut . . .
REDCAP	Blade bites into bone . . .
MORGAN	Steel finds its home . . .
MERRY	In heart and liver . . .
HANDS	And stomach and throat . . .
HUNTER	And all is confusion . . .
TRELAWNEY	All's lost in a world of confusion . . .
JIM	No sense or meaning . . .
CHORUS 3	Just cut and slash . . .
GREY	Slice and stab . . .
CHORUS 4	Bite and kick . . .
JOYCE	And tear and rip . . .
CHORUS 5	And everything about us is falling apart!
	(CHORUS 5 goes. Others also go after they speak.)
CHORUS 6	The whole world tumbling about our ears . . .
REDCAP	And some of us are dead . . .
DICK	And some of us are running . . .
MORGAN	We don't know where, just running blind . . .
MERRY	Clutching the scraps and rags of our lives . . .
HANDS	For it's come to no good and we've had enough!

30

40

(The drumbeat stops. SILVER, who has been watching all this, cries out.)

SILVER Come back! Where are you going? Come back, I say! Run, and I'll run you through!

(CHORUS 3 and 4 go.) 50

You lily-livered dogs! Desert, will you? Is this the kind of scum I brought along with me? You call yourselves men! I'll show you what a man is! I'll be dancing on corpses before I'm through! I'm not finished nor done with yet!

(SILVER goes. The rest go after they speak.)

GREY At last it's over.

JOYCE Finished and done with.

HUNTER Nothing remains but a terrible silence . . .

SMOLLETT And the drifting smoke . . .

LIVESEY And the fading sunlight . . . 60

TRELAWNEY As the island settles back into stillness . . .

JIM And we that are left, look round at what's left.

(All have gone. Only ADULT JIM remains.)

ARTWORK AND WRITING The fight is staged in a completely 'non-naturalistic' way, with the characters narrating the action. In pairs, discuss how you might stage this scene for the theatre.
  ● How and where would you place the actors?
  ● What would you do, to make the scene as exciting as possible?
After your discussion, make a sketch of your ideas for this scene, with notes explaining what would be happening onstage.

CHARACTER AND WRITING What do you think the characters' feelings are immediately after the fight? Three men have been killed, one of them the Squire's long-time servant, Hunter, who has died in agony. Imagine you're one of the survivors in the moments just after the fight, and write down your thoughts and feelings as a monologue, in prose or poetry.

ACT 3 ❖ SCENE 6

ADULT JIM steps forward and speaks to the audience.

ADULT JIM   The pirates had retreated. The day was ours. Five of their   1
men lay dead on the ground. Ours we buried – Grey, Joyce
and Hunter, who'd been wounded in the stomach, and
whose release was the end of a long, slow agony. This was
our victory, and it sickened me. All I wanted was to get
away, escape from the heat and the smell of blood. And so,
as evening fell, unnoticed by the others, I took a pistol,
stole out of the stockade, slipped over the fence, and went
out into the dying light of the island.

(HANDS enters, with a bottle, and speaks to the audience.)   10

HANDS   And comes at last to me, his worst nightmare, on board the
old ship, *Hispaniola*.

*(He takes a swig from the bottle, and drinks throughout the
following.)*

After our fight at the stockade – and after what was left of
us had re-grouped – Silver sent me back on board. He
wanted somebody here in case Smollett tried to take her
again and leave us stranded. So, with the rest of them
camped on the shore, and making merry of it, here stands
I alone, Israel Hands, man and master of the ship. And here   20
I finds many a bottle of rum and port and brandy in the
Captain's cabin. So I says to myself, 'Israel,' I says, 'you're
captain now, and you may as well take all the advantages of
your rank.' Which is what I proceed to do. And soon the
sun's gone down and it's dark. And I don't much care, 'cos
by now I'm dreaming myself rolling on a bed of doubloons
and guineas and louis-d'ors – and I'm happy as Adam when
he first woke in Eden – when all of a sudden the ship gives
a jolt – and the deck rolls under me – *(He falls to his knees.)*

– and I'm falling sideways – and I knocks my head – and   30
I'm on my knees, and there's blood in my eyes . . .

(JIM enters, with a pistol, pointed at HANDS.)

. . . and when I wipe that blood away, curse me if there
ain't that boy, Jim Hawkins, in front of me, like something
crawled up out of the deep.

JIM	Stay as you are, Mr Hands.
HANDS	Where'd you spring from, by thunder!
JIM	I've come aboard to take possession of this ship – and you'll regard me as your captain until further notice.
HANDS	Will I, now? 40
JIM	Yes, Mr Hands. You will.
HANDS	It seems I must, then, as you've got the upper-hand of Israel Hands, so to speak. And seeing as you seem to have cut us adrift into the bargain.
JIM	You're right, Mr Hands, that's exactly what I have done.
HANDS	Silver was right. You're a lad to be reckoned with, you are.
JIM	Smart as paint, Mr Hands.
HANDS	Aye, that's true. But smart enough to walk across water? I doubt it. Though where in the fires of hell you got yourself a boat from beats me. 50
JIM	Never mind about that. As I say, I've taken possession of this ship, and I mean to sail her away from this anchorage around to the North Inlet, and beach her there.
HANDS	To be sure you do!

doubloons and guineas and louis d'ors *Different types of coin.*

JIM	With your help, of course.
HANDS	Of course! What choice do I have? With that pistol pointed at me, I'd help you sail her up to Execution Dock, so I would, if you was to give the word!
JIM	The North Inlet will do, Mr Hands. Jump to it!
HANDS	Aye, aye – Captain Hawkins.

(HANDS stands, slowly, as JIM keeps the pistol trained on him. He takes a rope, hauls on it, as if turning a sail, lashes it fast, then takes the wheel. While this happens, ADULT JIM narrates.)

ADULT JIM	After I'd left the stockade, I'd seen the pirates take the longboat out to the ship, and return to make their camp on the beach. It came to me then that if the ship were to somehow be cut free, and taken to another part of the island, it might do them some harm and us some good. So I made my way to the White Rock, and found Ben Gunn's boat there, and took it out. I could hear someone singing to himself on deck as I clung to the hawser and sawed it through, strand by strand, with my knife. But then, as the ship broke free from anchor, it lurched to one side, and a sudden wave swept the wild man's boat away. I was left hanging on to the rope, so there was nothing to do but climb aboard, and take my chances with Israel Hands.

(ISRAEL HANDS starts to sing.)

HANDS	Fifteen men on a dead man's chest Yo Ho Ho . . .
JIM	No more of that, if you please, Mr Hands. It's not a song that's much to my liking.
HANDS	As you say – Captain Hawkins. Though it's a pity a man

---

 hawser *Another name for the ship's cable, by which the anchor was secured.*

	can't pass the time with singing out a stave or two.	
JIM	The time will pass soon enough.	
HANDS	You're in the right of it. A pleasant voyage this is, to be sure. We've a good wind and a strong current, and there's the sun rising already and our destination in sight.	
JIM	Where?	
HANDS	There, to the port bow.	

(JIM looks to where HANDS is pointing.) 90

ADULT JIM	Lit by the dawn-light, I saw wooded slopes running down to the shoreline, the glint of a river, a narrow beach.	
HANDS	We can ship her in there. Beach her, and tie a line round one of them trees.	
ADULT JIM	And, tangled among the overhanging roots and branches, the ruin of a great ship, blooming with flowers, that had taken root on her decks.	
HANDS	Wrecked in some storm, no doubt, and now she returns to that which she come from. As do we all, Master Hawkins, when our time comes round.	100

*(HANDS has left the wheel and is moving towards JIM.
JIM turns and sees him.)*

JIM	Back to your place, Mr Hands. Guide her in.	
HANDS	No need to fear. I was just getting myself a drink. My throat's dry as sawdust.	
JIM	There'll be time enough for that when we're ashore.	
HANDS	Deny a man a drink, would you? You're a hard master, to be sure. But maybe not so hard as to pass me a bottle so's I can take a swig at the wheel.	
JIM	Very well. I'll do that for you.	110
HANDS	There's one there, at your feet.	

(*JIM picks up the bottle.*)

JIM   It's almost empty.

HANDS   There's enough to oil my throat.

(*He holds out one hand for the bottle. JIM passes it to him.*)

120

JIM   Here you are.

HANDS   Thank you kindly – Captain Hawkins!

(*As HANDS reaches out, he hits JIM's arm, knocking him round. JIM drops the bottle and the pistol, with a cry. He turns to make for the pistol, but HANDS grabs him, at the same time drawing a knife and putting it to his throat.*)

13●

HANDS   A pleasant voyage this is! And made pleasanter still by the cutting of your throat . . . !

(*JIM elbows HANDS in the stomach, and manages to twist free. He dives across the deck, grabs the pistol, and swings round to face HANDS.*)

JIM   Keep back!

HANDS   Or else what? You'll shoot me will you?

JIM   Don't doubt it!

HANDS   But I do, Jim Hawkins, I do doubt it.

(*He advances on JIM throughout the following, and JIM backs away, climbing up to the central raised area.*)

140

JIM	You'd best not to!
HANDS	It's something to kill a man close up, you see. When he's looking you in the face, and you can feel his breath on you, and see the light of life burning in his eyes. You has to have the stomach for it. And what I asks myself is – has you? And what I answers is – no you haven't, nor ever will.
JIM	Not another step, Mr Hands, or you can say your prayers!
HANDS	Now what would a man like me be doing saying his prayers? What would he pray for, and who would he pray to? Him being a man without God, and his soul already in hell!

150

(They are both on the raised level now, HANDS facing JIM.)

JIM	One more step, Mr Hands, and I'll blow your brains out!
HANDS	Jim, we've fouled, you and me, and I'll have to strike. Dead men don't bite, that's my prayer. And amen, I say, and so be it!

(HANDS raises his knife to stab down at JIM. JIM cries out.)

(They both freeze. Pause.)

(HANDS lowers the knife, looses it, turns from JIM, makes his way down from the raised area, speaks to the audience.)

160

HANDS	And there's a sound of thunder and a flash of light, and I'm falling, falling through that light, falling so slow it seems to take forever, and there's only the wind singing and the bright light blazing. And then it's cold water and the waves roaring, and the dark of the deep, and nothing more.

(JIM looks down at HANDS.)

JIM	Dead men don't bite.

(HANDS walks off.)

DISCUSSION In this scene, for the first time in the play, Jim takes direct action. As a class, discuss why you think he takes action now?
- What prompts him to take command of the ship, and risk his life against Israel Hands?
- How has his character changed from the start of the play?

ACTING From the start of this scene, you can tell that the action is building towards a showdown between Israel Hands and Jim. Because Jim is narrating the story, we are more or less certain that Israel Hands will die.

What makes it an interesting scene for an audience to watch, is the build-up of the tension between Jim and Hands, leading to the moment when the showdown takes place.

In pairs, try acting out this scene, and see what different ways you can find, in the way the characters speak and act, to build up tension in the scene.

WRITING Jim has killed a man. Write down his thoughts and feelings, as a monologue in prose or poetry, as he gazes at Israel Hands' body floating in the sea.

ACT 3 ❖ SCENE 7

SILVER enters, and speaks to ADULT JIM. As he does, BOY JIM comes down from the raised area.

SILVER	Aye. It's true, Jim. Dead men don't bite. There's the creed we live by, and you learned it that day, for sure. But how did you feel, eh, as you looked down from that masthead there, and saw him lying face down in the water, dead as cold pork, meat for the fishes? How did that strike you, Jim? And how did it strike me when I learned it was you that done it, and took our ship and left us high and dry!	1

(He turns quickly and grabs JIM. JIM cries out.)

Look, here, lads! Look who it is we've here caught ourselves!

(MORGAN, MERRY and DICK enter, as ADULT JIM narrates.) 10

ADULT JIM	And caught I was! For after mooring the ship and returning to the stockade, I'd found, not my friends, there, but Silver and his men!	
SILVER	Here's Jim Hawkins, dropped in to see us, all friendly-like!	
JIM	What are you doing here? Where are the others? What have you done to them?	
MORGAN	Sent them to hell – where you can join them if you like –	
SILVER	Batten your hatches, Tom Morgan, till you're spoke to!	
JIM	Are they dead?	
SILVER	No, Jim. You've no need to fear on your friends' account.	20

batten your hatches *In literal terms, this means to batten down, or fasten, the hatches over a hold on board ship. Silver uses the term to mean 'shut up'.*

JIM	Then where are they? And why are you here?
SILVER	It makes a good tale, Jim, and a strange one, too. And I'll be glad to tell it to you. For I've always liked you, I have, for a lad of spirit, and the picture of my own self when I was young and handsome. *(He turns to DICK.)* Dick. Bring up one of them boxes for Jim Hawkins, so's he can sit and take his ease.
MERRY	Let him bring his own.
SILVER	I reckon he'd best do as I tell him, George Merry! I'm captain here, not you!

30

(DICK brings a box. JIM sits. SILVER remains standing. The others stand back, observing.)

Now, Jim. Here it is. Early in the morning down comes Doctor Livesey with a flag of truce, asking to make a bargain. And I sees straight away I has to make one with him, for there's the ship gone, and some of my lads a-lying where they slept with their throats cut.

MORGAN	If I was to lay hands on the devil that done that . . .
SILVER	Stow it, George. Let me finish my tale. *(To JIM.)* So, I asks the Doctor what kind of bargain it is he's looking for, and he offers us the stoockade, here, with provisions, in return for free passage for him and the rest.

40

JIM	A free passage? Where to?
SILVER	That I don't know, Jim, and he made it plain it wasn't my business to ask. But the upshot of it is, they've tramped, and here we are. And here you are, Jim, and it seems to me you'd best throw in your lot with us. For the Doctor and his friends have washed their hands of you.

stow it *To stow is to store something away. Again, Silver means 'shut up'.*

JIM	What do you mean?
SILVER	When I asks after you, he tells me you've taken off again. **50** Don't know where you are, and don't care. 'We're about sick of him,' he says. Aye, them were his words, Jim. Meaning he's took against you. But not me. You're a smart one, Jim, and I always wanted you to join us and take your share, and now, by thunder, here's your chance! What do you say, Jim? Will you join with us?
JIM	I know you, Silver, and what to expect of you. I've seen too many die since I fell in with you. And if the worst's to come, then let it. For it's little I care now.
SILVER	Brave words, lad. Say on. **60**
JIM	Here you are, in a bad way. Ship lost, treasure lost, men lost. Your whole business gone to wreck. And if you want the truth of it – if you want to know who did it – it was I!
MERRY	Eh? What's that the boy's saying . . . ?
JIM	I was in the hold the night we sighted land – I heard you – you, Silver, and you, Dick Johnson, and Israel Hands – I heard all that you planned and told every word you said before the hour was out!
DICK	By heaven . . . !
JIM	And as for the ship, it was I cut her cable, and took her **70** where you'll see her no more – and I who sent Israel Hands to the bottom of the sea.
MORGAN	He'll pay for that, if nothing else!
JIM	Kill me, if you like, or spare me. If you spare me, then bygones are bygones, and when you're brought to justice, I'll do my best to save you from the gallows.
MERRY	Kill him, I say. It was him that knowed Black Dog in the *Spyglass*.
MORGAN	And him that had the chart from Billy Bones!

SILVER	Aye. So it was, and so it is. First and last, it seems, we've split upon Jim Hawkins!

80

MERRY	Here's an end to it, then!

(He draws a knife, steps forward. SILVER turns on him.)

SILVER Hold, there! Who are you, George Merry? Maybe you thought you was captain here! By the powers, I'll teach you better! Cross me, and you'll go where many a better man's gone before!

(MERRY and SILVER confront each other, neither backing down.)

DICK George is in the right of it, John.

SILVER Is he, now? And is that what you say, Tom Morgan?

90

MORGAN I reckon it is. We won't be hazed by you, John Silver.

SILVER So that's the way of it! Well, then! Which of you fine gentlemen of fortune will take me on! Step forward! Take a cutlass, him that dares, and I'll see the colour of his insides!

MERRY We ain't looking for a fight, John . . .

DICK All we wants is to have our say . . .

SILVER You don't have no say! I'm Captain here by election, and it's me that has the say-so or no!

MORGAN We have our rights!

SILVER Do you, now? And what rights be they?

100

MERRY Rights according to rules. Seamen's council.

SILVER Ah, George Merry. I see what's in your mind. But I'm not one to go against ship's rules. Go on, then. Have your council.

(MERRY, MORGAN and DICK draw aside. SILVER speaks urgently to JIM.)

SILVER Now, look here, Jim Hawkins. You're within half a plank of

| | death. They mean to throw me off, but I'll stand by you, for I knows you're the right sort. I'm your last card, Jim, and, by thunder, you're mine. | 110 |

JIM   What do you mean?

SILVER   I mean all's lost, Jim. Soon as I seen the ship gone, I knowed the game was up. I'm the Squire's man, now, and I'll save you from them fools and their council. But, it's tit-for-tat, Jim. You swear to save Long John from swinging.

JIM   All right. I promise I'll do what I can.

SILVER   It's a bargain! Now it's back to back, and face the worst grinning.

(During the above, DICK has torn a page from a small book, MERRY has written on it, and given it to MORGAN. They now turn to SILVER.)   120

MORGAN   John . . .

SILVER   Step up, Tom Morgan. I won't eat you. I know the rules. Hand it over.

(MORGAN hands the paper to SILVER.)

The Black Spot! I thought so! But this come from a Bible? What fool's gone and cut up a Bible!

MORGAN   It was Dick that done it!

SILVER   You was it, Dick Johnson? You've seen your last slice of luck, lad, you may lay to that!   130

MERRY   Belay that talk, John Silver! This crew has tipped you the Black Spot. Now just you turn it over and see what's writ there.

SILVER   Thank you for reminding my of my dooty, George. You always was brisk for business. Let's see then. *(He turns the page, reads 'Deposed'.)*

MERRY   Aye. That's it, John. Deposed.

SILVER	And very pretty writ, too. Your hand, is it, George? You're getting quite a leading man in this here crew, ain't you? You'll be captain next, I shouldn't wonder. 140
MERRY	Maybe – if that's what's elected for.
SILVER	Meanwhile you ain't Captain yet, George Merry. I am – till you've laid out your charges and I've answered them.
MERRY	I can lay them out clear enough. First, you've made a hash of this voyage. Second, you let enemy out of this here trap for nothing. And third, there's the boy.
SILVER	Is that all?
MERRY	It's enough.
SILVER	Here's my answer, then. I made hash of this cruise, did I? If things had been left as I'd wanted them, we'd be aboard 150 ship, now, with all the treasure, and every man alive. But who was it had to start the killing the day we landed, and show our hand before time? Why, it was you, George Merry and Israel Hands, and you, Tom Morgan!
MORGAN	I was against that from the start! I said so to you, George!
SILVER	As for the boy, isn't he a hostage? He might be our last chance of saving our necks. But that wouldn't occur to you, would it, George? You was never one for laying a clear course.
DICK	When it comes to that, what about you letting the enemy 160 go? There didn't seem much clear thinking in that.
SILVER	That's what you say, is it, Master Johnson? Didn't I say I'd made a bargain with them? And don't a bargain have two sides to it?
MERRY	We seen their side of it, sure enough, but I'll be damned if I can see ours!
SILVER	Then damned you be for a blind fool! See what your eyes can make of this!

(He takes out the chart from his pocket.)

MERRY   Let me see! 170

(He takes it. The other two gather round him.)

MORGAN   That's Flint, sure enough! There's his initials – J.F.

SILVER   Now you can take it and find the treasure for yourselves.
For I'm sick to heart at the lot of you, and I resign. Elect
who you please to be your captain! I'm done with it!

MORGAN   Where's the sense of that? We've got our captain! John's
found us the treasure, and my vote's for him.

MERRY   He might have found us the treasure, but how are we going
to get away with it, with no ship?

DICK   He'll get us the ship back, if any man can. John Silver for 180
captain, I say!

SILVER   Well, George, I reckon you'll have to wait another turn.
And as for this Black Spot, it ain't much good, now. Here,
Jim. Keep it for a curiosity.

(He gives JIM the paper, turns to the others.)

And now that's all settled, let's set ourselves to the task in
hand. We'll find the treasure, and, once we have it, I reckon
Jim here'll tell us where he's put the ship. And once we
have that – it's a fair wind to a far shore, and a future
crowned with gold! 190

*(MERRY, MORGAN and DICK take up shovels, picks, muskets,
and so on. SILVER speaks softly to JIM.)*

And you and me, Jim, we must stick together, back to back.
For I don't know what we're walking into, but we'll save
our necks in the face of fortune and fate.

*(SILVER turns from JIM, and prepares for the journey. As he does
so, ADULT JIM narrates.)*

ADULT JIM   So we set off into the unknown – and the paper he gave me, I have still. A page from the Bible, blackened and torn, and, where the mark was scratched, these words standing out . . .

200

JIM 'Without are dogs and murderers.'

ACTING Silver tells Jim how Doctor Livesey came that morning to make a bargain with him.

In small groups, act out this scene between the Doctor and Silver. Other pirates can also be in the scene. Use the information from Silver's speech to help create the scene.

HOT SEATING In small groups, one takes on the role of Jim, and the others try to find out from him why he told Silver and the others that he was the cause of all their troubles, when he knew this action would endanger his life.

Then, one takes on the role of Silver, and the others find out from him why he decided to defend Jim, even though this would lead to trouble, and why he kept the fact that he had the map secret right until he had been deposed.

CHARACTER AND WRITING In small groups, discuss the different characters of the three pirates: Tom Morgan, George Merry and Dick.
- How are they similar?
- How are they different?
- Which of them presents the greatest danger to Silver and Jim.
After this, write brief character sketches of the three.

ARTWORK Storyboard four events from this scene, as if you were making a film. As before, sketch the scenes in frames, and make notes on what would be heard, and what the camera would be doing.

ACT 3 ❖ SCENE 8

SILVER, JIM, MERRY, MORGAN and DICK now face the audience, standing a little apart. CHORUS enters, as voices of the jungle.

1st VOICE	They set off in the hot mid-morning . . .	1
2nd VOICE	Moving through marshy ground, tangled woodland . . .	
3rd VOICE	Their only guide a dead man's hand . . .	
4th VOICE	Flint's words speaking from beyond the grave . . .	
5th VOICE	'Tall tree, Spy-Glass shoulder . . .	
6th VOICE	'Bearing a point to the North of nor'-nor'-east.'	
SILVER	That way, lads. The plateau, there. That's the place we start from, I reckon.	
1st VOICE	Now the ground rises and clears about them . . .	
2nd VOICE	Slopes steadily upward to the hill's crest . . .	10
3rd VOICE	The air clearer, scent of broom and pine . . .	
4th VOICE	The light sharper as they near the summit . . .	
5th VOICE	And find Flint's marker lying before them . . .	
6th VOICE	The bones of a dead man stretched on the grass.	
DICK	Look! Do you see it?	
MORGAN	I see it, right enough.	
MERRY	A seaman. You can tell by his clothes.	
SILVER	Like enough. And see how he lies. Not in no natural way. He's been laid out, arms above his head, and feet and hands tied.	20
DICK	Like he was put there on purpose.	
SILVER	And so he was. If I'm not wrong, it was Flint done this.	

MORGAN	Flint!
MERRY	Six he brought with him, and he come back alone.
SILVER	And left one of them here stretched out as a compass, guiding the way to our Pole Star. See the way his arms are pointing? Straight to that tree on the hillside there!
MORGAN	You're right, John. But, by the powers – to think of him here – doing this – it chills me to the heart!
MERRY	I saw him dead. Billy took me in. There he laid, with the penny-pieces on his eyes.
MORGAN	He died bad, did Flint. Raging and hollering, and singing sometimes. 'Fifteen men' were his only song. And I've never rightly liked to hear it since.
SILVER	You praise your stars he is dead, mates, and not here with us, now. For it'd go hard for us if he was.
1st VOICE	And as they stand there on the crest of the ridge . . .
2nd VOICE	With the dead man's bones shining white in the sunlight . . .
3rd VOICE	And Flint's shadow lying cold in their hearts . . .
4th VOICE	They hear a sound lifting . . .
5th VOICE	A thin voice trembling . . .
6th VOICE	Ghost words rising out of the earth!
	(Off, a GHOST VOICE sings.)
GHOST VOICE	Fifteen men on a dead man's chest Yo-Ho-Ho and a bottle of rum!
DICK	Hear that? Did you all hear that?
MORGAN	I heard it! It come from the trees over there!
GHOST VOICE	Drink and the devil had done for the rest Yo-Ho-Ho and a bottle of rum!

30

40

50

DICK	There it is again!	60
MERRY	It's Flint! That's who it is! Flint!	
SILVER	Stow that! It ain't Flint! Flint's dead!	
MORGAN	Aye, but if ever a spirit was to walk, it'd be Flint's. And with us after his treasure . . .	
SILVER	Enough, Tom Morgan! That voice belongs to somebody flesh and blood . . .	
	(The GHOST VOICE calls out.)	
GHOST VOICE	Darby M'Graw! Darby M'Graw! Bring me rum. Rum, Darby M'Graw!	
MERRY	Flesh and blood, is it, Silver? Them was Flint's last words!	70
MORGAN	And who but us on this island knows them? Except Flint himself?	
	(The GHOST VOICE calls again.)	
GHOST VOICE	Darby M'Graw!	
DICK	That fixes it! I'm off . . . !	
	(DICK goes to run. SILVER grabs him.)	
SILVER	Belay there! Feared of Flint, are you? Feared of Flint's spirit? Well, I was never feared of Flint when he was alive, and, by the powers, I'll face him dead!	
	(He calls out.)	80
	You hear me, Flint, if that is you? This is John Silver talking! Barbecue! And what I have to say to you is this! I'm here to get that treasure, and get it I will, and I'll not be beat to it by man nor ghost nor devil!	

Darby M'Graw *Obviously one of Flint's crew.*

(Pause. There is silence.)

I reckon that's silenced him. Come on, lads. There's dollars waiting for us.

(CHORUS narrates)

1st VOICE	They walk on, and fear walks with them . . .
2nd VOICE	Fear like a fever possessing their bodies . . .
3rd VOICE	Urging them on, hurrying, stumbling . . .
4th VOICE	Towards the place where their dream lies shining . . .
5th VOICE	A glittering hoard, a dragon's cache . . .
6th VOICE	The buried sum of their lives' longing.
SILVER	This is the place, lads! We're here! This is where old Flint buried his treasure!
1st VOICE	They run forward . . .
2nd VOICE	Their eyes are burning . . .
3rd VOICE	Like hounds at the kill . . .
4th VOICE	Hungry, slavering . . .
5th VOICE	Pull up sharp, stare, dead in their tracks . . .
6th VOICE	At the empty hole in the broken earth.

(All stare downward in horror.)

MORGAN	It's gone! It's all gone!
DICK	Somebody's already been here!
MERRY	And they've taken it all.

(They drop to their knees, scrape at the ground with their fingers. CHORUS now leave on their lines.0

1st VOICE	Then they're down in the hole . . .
2nd VOICE	They're down on their knees . . .

90

100

11

3rd VOICE	They're digging the earth with raw fingers . . .
4th VOICE	Like men who had everything, and now they've lost it . . .
5th VOICE	Scratching among the broken boxes . . .
6th VOICE	Picking the bones of their hollow dream.

(*MERRY holds up a single coin.*)

MERRY Two guineas! A two guinea-piece! (*He stands, faces SILVER.*) That's your treasure, is it? You that never bungled nothing!

SILVER Dig away, boys. You'll find some pig-nuts there, I shouldn't wonder.

MERRY Do you hear him, mates? Hear how he laughs at us? He knew it all along! He's sold us out! Look in his face, and you'll see it!   120

SILVER Standing for captain again, are you, George Merry?

(*MORGAN and DICK are standing now.*)

MERRY There's just the two of them, mates. One's a boy, and one's an old cripple, and I mean to have the heart of both of them!

(*MERRY is about to attack SILVER when SMOLLETT, LIVESEY and TRELAWNEY enter, armed.*)

SMOLLETT Stay there! Hold!   130

TRELAWNEY One move and you're dead men!

SMOLLETT Now. Drop your weapons.

(*MERRY, MORGAN and DICK do so.*)

LIVESEY Jim. Come over here!

(*JIM begins to move towards LIVESEY. As he does so, MERRY grabs hold of him.*)

MERRY Hold your fire! You wouldn't want the boy harmed, would you? Dick. Tom. Take to your heels.

(DICK and MORGAN turn and run.)

Ah, but if only I had a knife on me, now, boy, I'd cut your throat in front of all your fine friends!   140

(He pushes JIM away from him, turns and runs off. Immediately, SILVER draws his pistol and fires. There is a pause.)

SILVER Well, George. I reckoned I settled you.

TRELAWNEY After the others . . . !

LIVESEY No. Leave them. We won't find them, now. And they're not likely to do us any harm.

SILVER Right enough. The only harm them poor lads are likely to do now is to theirselves. You came in about the nick of time, Doctor, for me and Hawkins. Saved our skins, you did,   150 and I thank you kindly for it.

TRELAWNEY It was Jim's skin we were looking to save, Silver. Not yours. Had he not been with you, we'd have cut you all to ribbons.

SILVER My compliments to you, Squire, but you'd have lost a true man, if you had. Isn't that right, Jim?

SMOLLETT A true man?

SILVER That's right, Captain Smollett, sir. And here he stands. John Silver, reporting for dooty.

(He salutes. As he does so, BEN GUNN enters behind him.)   160

BEN GUNN John Silver, says he. Reporting for duty, says he.
And where's all the booty, says he? Gone! says I.

(SILVER turns to him.)

SILVER Ben Gunn!

BEN GUNN Ben Gunn, as ever was. Or maybe Old Flint. *(He calls.)* Darby M'Graw! Darby M'Graw!

SILVER I knew I'd heard the voice before. And the treasure . . . !

BEN GUNN	The treasure, says you. Who took it, says you? Who searched for it these three years? Who found it and dug it up, and carried it back, long, weary journeys, to his cave? Ben Gunn, says I! Poor, lonely Ben Gunn! King of the Island! How do, Mr Silver? says I. Pretty well, thank you, says you.	170
SILVER	Ben Gunn. To think it was you as done for me.	
	(He takes a step towards BEN. BEN scuttles back, scared.)	
SMOLLETT	That's enough, Silver!	
SILVER	Begging your pardon, Captain. But it's hard for a man like me to be taken broadside on by a man like Ben Gunn.	
LIVESEY	*(To JIM.)* After you told me about Ben, I went to see him. He showed me where he'd put the treasure. I knew then we had no more need of the map, so we handed it over, and laid our trap. And if you hadn't taken yourself off again . . .	180
JIM	They wouldn't have lost the ship! It was I that took it. And I know where it is.	
TRELAWNEY	Bless me! And to think of all the things you said about him, Livesey! The boy's a hero!	
SILVER	Smart as paint, Squire. I've always said it.	
	(TRELAWNEY turns on SILVER.)	
TRELAWNEY	As for, sir, you are a villain! And when we return I shall see that you're brought to trial for mutiny and murder and hanged from the highest gibbet!	190
JIM	No, Mr Trelawney. You can't. He saved my life, you see, and I promised I'd save him. I gave him my word.	
	(Pause.)	

gibbet *A gallows.*

TRELAWNEY   Then, let it be. But you have much to account for in the next world, Silver, and the dead hang like millstones round your neck.

SILVER   Thank you, kindly, Squire. It's a weight I must bear . . . and as for the next world – I'm willing to take my chances.

SMOLLETT   Gentlemen, we're done here. I suggest we return to the cave, find the longboats, and begin loading the treasure aboard. Then, at last, we can leave this wretched place, and make our voyage home.   200

BEN GUNN   This way! Follow me! I know the way. Follow Ben Gunn, Captain Silver, and he'll show you your treasure. He'll show you Flint's heart, cut out and cooked by poor Ben Gunn! For a piece of cheese, my lads! For a piece of English cheese!

(BEN GUNN runs off. The rest follow him, except for JIM.)

DISCUSSION As a class, discuss why you think the pirates are so ready to believe that the voice they hear is that of Flint's ghost. What condition are they in, physically and mentally, that might make them likely to believe in Flint's ghost?

ARTWORK/WRITING Scene 8 involves a journey through different kinds of landscape. The voices describe these landscapes for us, but how would you represent such a journey onstage? Make notes on how you might do this, and draw a sketch of the characters onstage for this scene.

WRITING Although Jim is present throughout this scene, he hardly speaks. Write down his thoughts and feelings as a monologue, in prose or poetry, as he makes the journey, up to the point where they discover that the treasure is gone.

ACTING Livesey tells Silver how he went to meet Ben Gunn, and how Ben showed them where he'd put the treasure. This was the reason they were willing to give up the map and the stockade. In small groups, create one of the following scenes:
  1 The meeting between Livesey and Ben Gunn
  2 Livesey telling the Squire and Captain Smollett about Ben Gunn and the treasure.

DISCUSSION In small groups, discuss what you think Ben Gunn means when he says: 'He'll show you Flint's heart, cut out and cooked by poor Ben Gunn. For a piece of cheese, my lads!'. Share your thoughts and ideas with the other groups.

ACT 3 ❖ SCENE 9

JIM stands central. ADULT JIM enters to one side.

ADULT JIM   And there, in the cave, at last I saw it – the thing we had   1
come for, and suffered for – and that so many men had
given their lives for – Billy Bones, Blind Pew, Israel Hands,
George Merry – them and countless more besides. And the
spirits of those dead men hovered in the dark, and their
voices whispered, as I gazed in wonder at Flint's treasure.

(CHORUS enters, and stands around JIM.)

1st VOICE   Gleaming in the darkness, a golden fire . . .

2nd VOICE   Doubloons, guineas, pieces of eight . . .

3rd VOICE   A lifetime's bounty . . .   10

4th VOICE   Like cold flames flickering . . .

5th VOICE   The loot of the world . . .

6th VOICE   The heart's dark desire.

(SILVER enters, on the other side of JIM.)

SILVER Men must die, Jim. Some in their beds, some as beggars in gutters. We all risk something. And what better to risk it for than this, eh? Gold! Fortune! Money in your pocket, the sweat of the sun in your fist! And you'll take your share of it, won't you, Jim? You and the Doctor, and the Squire, Captain Smollett and old Ben Gunn, you'll all take your share. And, by thunder, I'll take mine! 20

ADULT JIM It was evening, and we'd been three days at sea, heading for the nearest port in Spanish America, to take on provisions and extra hands. He came and stood beside me on the deck, talking free and easy, as in the early days of our voyage out, and I thought he seemed happier and his heart lighter than in the time that had gone before. Then he fell silent, and for a while we both stood gazing at the gentle waters splashed with the rays of the setting sun. Then I turned to speak to him, and he was gone. And that was the last of him. For he took a sack of coins to help him in his wanderings, and I've never seen or heard of him in this world again. 30

(During the above, SILVER has turned and gone. JIM turns, sees he is alone, then walks to the back of the stage, and sits down among the crates and boxes. He sleeps. Others enter on their lines.)

MORGAN We two they left on the island, and in truth, Flint's spirit did walk there . . .

DICK For we were dead within two months, of the fever and a cut throat. 40

TRELAWNEY As for the rest of us, we returned home richer than when we'd set out . . .

LIVESEY Living the rest of our lives out in comfort and ease . . .

SMOLLETT As gentlemen should, who've earned their wealth.

BEN GUNN	Except for Ben Gunn. He spent his thousand pound in nineteen days, and was back again begging on the twentieth.
MRS HAWKINS	And Mrs Hawkins thanked God for her son's safe return, and to see him grow to such a fine, well-bred gentleman. 50
ADULT JIM	And I live as a gentleman still, in a fine house, in the city, far from the land's edge and out of sight of the sea. For oxen and ropes wouldn't bring me back there again. But still, at night, I dream.
1st VOICE	And he hears the surf booming . . .
2nd VOICE	And the birds shrieking . . .
3rd VOICE	Slap of sail in the wind . . .
4th VOICE	The roll of the deep . . .
5th VOICE	And on the edge of the world a lone figure stands . . .
6th VOICE	And a voice rings out between sky and sea . . . 60
SILVER	Wake, lad! It's all here. Out in the world with Long John! All you ever dreamed of! Gold! Fortune! The sweat of the sun! Doubloons and dollars and pieces of eight!

(Lights to blackout.)

(The end.)

FREEZE-FRAME In groups, freeze-frame the moment when the characters stand, gazing at the treasure. Each character speaks aloud their thoughts and feelings at that particular moment.

DISCUSSION As a class, discuss how you think Silver manages to steal some of the treasure and escape from the ship. Does he do this alone, or does he have help? If you think he has help, who helps him, and why?

ACTING In twos, or more, create the scene where Jim and his mother meet again. There may be other characters from the play in this scene.

ARTWORK Imagine you're making a film. What would your closing shot be? Sketch the shot in a frame, showing what you want the audience to see.

Make notes on what sounds or dialogue they might hear over this image. Think carefully about what effect you want to create in this final image that the audience would take away with them.

CHARACTER Complete your character file by adding to it any characters who have only appeared in this Act, and adding to those notes you already have.

LOOKING BACK AT THE PLAY

1 Discussion: Language

There are several kinds of stage-language used in the play: straightforward dialogue, single-person narration, and chorus narration. Find examples in the play of these different techniques, and discuss why you think the playwright decided to use them at those points.

How do these three kinds of stage-language differ from each other?

2 Writing: Silver's Story

Think about what might happen to Silver after he escapes from the ship.
- Where does he go?
- What other events might befall him?
- Does he live out the rest of his days quietly with his wife?

Make notes, and then use the notes to write an account of Silver's life after the story ends. Write this in the third person, or imagine you're Silver.

3 Artwork

Design a poster for a theatre production of this play.

4 Discussion: Greed

One of the major themes of the play is greed. Many of the characters in the play are driven by greed, and the desire for great wealth is behind all the action in the play.

As a class, discuss which characters in the play are driven chiefly by greed.
- Are there are any characters who have different motives?
- If you think there are, who are they, and what drives them?

Support these ideas with extracts from the play.

5 Writing: Character

From your character file, choose one character, and write a detailed description of them – what they're like, what action they're involved in, how they affect the action of the play, and, if they change through the course of the play, how they change.

6 Discussion: Silver's Character

In groups, discuss the character of John Silver.
- Is he really 'a devil from hell', as he is described?

● Would you say he's a good, or a bad character? Is he both, or neither?

● What is it that makes him such a powerful, and memorable character?

Find examples from the text to support your ideas. Then share your thoughts and ideas with the other groups.

7 Maps

Look at the map (page v) of the island, designed by Stevenson himself. See if you can use it to follow the action of the story on the island.

You could also try creating your own island map.

The island is supposed to be in the Caribbean. Using an atlas, see if you can chart the voyage of the *Hispaniola*.

8 Discussion: The Book and the Play

Read this extract from the novel, describing the killing of Israel Hands, then compare it with the same scene in the play. Then, as a class, discuss how the two are different, and how they're similar, and why you think the playwright wrote the scene in this way. Can you think of an alternative way of staging the scene?

The sudden canting of the ship had made the deck no place for running on; I had to find some new way of escape, and that upon the instant, for my foe was almost touching me. Quick as thought I sprang into the mizzen shrouds, rattled up hand over hand, and did not draw a breath till I was seated on the cross-trees.

I had been saved by being prompt; the dirk had struck not half a foot below me, as I pursued my upward flight; and there stood Israel Hands with his mouth open and his face upturned to mine; a perfect statue of surprise and disappointment.

Now that I had a moment to myself, I lost no time in changing the priming of my pistol, and then, having one ready for service, and to make assurance doubly sure, I proceeded to draw the load of the other, and recharge it afresh from the beginning.

My new employment struck Hands all of a heap; he began to see the dice going against him; and, after an obvious hesitation, he also hauled himself heavily into the shrouds, and, with the dirk in his teeth, began slowly and painfully to mount. It cost him no end of time and groans to haul his wounded leg behind him; and I had quietly finished my arrangements before he was much more than a third of the way up. Then, with a pistol in either hand, I addressed him.

'One more step, Mr Hands, ' said I, 'and I'll blow your brains out! Dead men don't bite, you know,' I added with a chuckle.

He stopped instantly. I could see by the working of his face that he was trying to think, and the process was so slow and laborious that, in my new-found security, I laughed aloud. At last, with a swallow or two, he spoke, his face still wearing the same expression of extreme perplexity. In order to speak he had to take the dagger from his mouth, but, in all else, he remained unmoved.

'Jim,' says he, 'I reckon we're fouled, you and me, and we'll have to sign articles.